Supervision in Psychoanalysis and Psychotherapy

Supervision in Psychoanalysis and Psychotherapy demonstrates why supervision is an essential component of any psychoanalytic or therapeutic work. Drawing on Winnicott and rich clinical material, and featuring work with Patrick Casement, this book provides new guidance on psychodynamic supervision and explores how its skilful use can have a significant effect on the outcome of such work, enabling the practitioner to rethink their theoretical approach, and thereby view issues differently in the clinical setting.

Built around the case study of a challenging but successful long-term individual therapy, *Supervision in Psychoanalysis and Psychotherapy* examines how clinicians can become 'stuck' in their work with certain patients, struggling to find a way to get through to them. Diana Shmukler brings together a fascinating combination of various perspectives, detailing the patient's own words, the therapists' views and reflections and the effect of a brief introduction to art therapy, whilst underlining the power and impact, both theoretically and practically, of using a different approach in supervision. Shmukler superbly integrates theory and practice, underlining the validity of a two-person psychology and the therapeutic relationship, whilst also illustrating the centrality of both participants' commitment to, and belief in, the process of therapy. Importantly, the book provides a clinical example in which the subjectivities of all the participants are shown to be clearly central to the work. Shmukler underlines the significance of supervision to complex cases, even that of a highly experienced therapist.

Supervision in Psychoanalysis and Psychotherapy will appeal to psychoanalysts and psychotherapists, students and trainees in integrative psychotherapy, counsellors and psychiatrists, as well as patients seeking help for deep-seated issues.

Diana Shmukler, Ph.D., is an integrative and relational psychotherapist, supervisor and trainer registered with the UKCP. She is a clinical psychologist with the Health Professions Council in the UK and South African Medical and Dental Council, as well as a training and supervising transactional analyst (TSTA). She is currently Visiting Professor at the Metanoia Institute in London, the University of Middlesex and also the University of Utrecht, Netherlands.

Supervision in Psychoanalysis and Psychotherapy

A case study and clinical guide

Diana Shmukler

LONDON AND NEW YORK

First published 2017
by Routledge
2 Park Square, Milton Park, Abingdon, Oxon OX14 4RN

and by Routledge
711 Third Avenue, New York, NY 10017

Routledge is an imprint of the Taylor & Francis Group, an informa business

© 2017 Diana Shmukler

The right of Diana Shmukler to be identified as author of this work has been asserted by her in accordance with sections 77 and 78 of the Copyright, Designs and Patents Act 1988.

All rights reserved. No part of this book may be reprinted or reproduced or utilised in any form or by any electronic, mechanical, or other means, now known or hereafter invented, including photocopying and recording, or in any information storage or retrieval system, without permission in writing from the publishers.

Trademark notice: Product or corporate names may be trademarks or registered trademarks, and are used only for identification and explanation without intent to infringe.

British Library Cataloguing in Publication Data
A catalogue record for this book is available from the British Library

Library of Congress Cataloging in Publication Data
Names: Shmukler, Diana, author.
Title: Supervision in psychoanalysis and psychotherapy : a case study and clinical guide / Diana Shmukler.
Description: Milton Park, Abingdon, Oxon ; New York, NY : Routledge, 2016. | Includes bibliographical references and index.
Identifiers: LCCN 2015049322| ISBN 9781138999725 (hbk) | ISBN 9781138999732 (pbk) | ISBN 9781315658094 (ebk)
Subjects: LCSH: Psychoanalysis--Study and teaching--Supervision. | Psychotherapy--Study and teaching--Supervision. | Psychotherapists--Supervision of.
Classification: LCC RC502 .S56 2016 | DDC 616.89/17076--dc23
LC record available at http://lccn.loc.gov/2015049322

ISBN: 978-1-138-99972-5 (hbk)
ISBN: 978-1-138-99973-2 (pbk)
ISBN: 978-1-315-65809-4 (ebk)

Typeset in Times New Roman
by Taylor & Francis Books

To my husband Meish for his love, forbearance and unfailing support

Contents

Acknowledgement		ix
Foreword by Patrick Casement		xi
Introduction		xiii
1	A search for a safe pair of hands	1
2	Little girl and better mother	37
3	The impact of the art therapy	45
4	The changing transference from idealisation to the failing mother	57
5	Supervision: finding the missing ingredient	69
6	The letters and their role in the therapy	83
7	Finishing the work: the final crisis and ending	103
8	Some of the theoretical ideas that supported the therapy	119
Afterword ANDREW SAMUELS		133
Bibliography		137
Index		139

Acknowledgement

My deepest gratitude and appreciation go to the two people without whom this book could not have been written.

To the patient, for her trust and faith in me and in the process of the work even when it seemed to be impossible.

To Patrick Casement, in the first place for his willingness to undertake the supervision and his recognition of the potential for a good outcome. And then for his invaluable belief in the possibility of publishing the work and extending himself to provide the support and encouragement necessary to bring it to fruition.

I am also grateful to Gill Hinshelwood for her meticulous, thorough and thoughtful editing which has added to the structure and organisation of the manuscript.

Over the years I have remained grateful to all those I have learnt so much from, particularly my patients, clients, students and supervisees.

Foreword by Patrick Casement

This book is an account of two different phases in a most unusual therapy. It tells us a lot about the difficulties, and potential, that can be encountered when working with a seriously deprived and disturbed patient: what works and what doesn't work.

The therapist here, Professor Diana Shmukler, came to me a lot of years ago, asking for urgent supervisory help with a patient she had already been seeing for two or three years. That earlier therapy had reached a point of crisis. Could I help her to find a way on with this (then really disturbed) patient?

Diana had, up to that time, been working within a humanistic and integrative framework, having believed that a form of re-parenting was what was most needed, and most likely to help, when a patient had been as severely deprived and disturbed throughout her childhood as this patient had been.

Following this belief, Diana had gone as far as any therapist could go, allowing this patient to regress to an early age, holding her, playing with her – agreeing to the patient's pleading that she be given many of the experiences that other children might take for granted, including being read children's stories, and much else.

Unfortunately, rather than resolving the inner disturbance of the patient, this attempt at meeting her demands had led only to an increase in these demands. It was almost as if nothing short of being adopted as the therapist's child would meet her thirst for re-parenting.

Alongside the considerable idealisation of the therapist as her 'new Mummy', most of the patient's intense disturbance remained located, unchanged, with her birth mother. Nothing seemed to shift that. It was for this reason that Diana came to me, asking for help to get through this complicated and intense tangle with her patient.

Diana had sensed, from my published work, that I might be able to help her to restore with this patient the clinical framework that was most needed, beyond that which the patient had created with her therapist – through the demands upon her and Diana's willingness (so far) to go along with those demands.

Through supervision we were able to re-establish a more viable framework, and the results were dramatic. The 'worst' in this patient's mind was, little by little, brought into the consulting room; her inner violence and the areas of madness in her mind, all of this and much more coming to be focused on her therapist. Along with this was a spate of handwritten letters, several in a single day, relentlessly subjecting Diana to all that the patient had assumed no-one could survive.

Throughout this terrible time I had to do all I could to help Diana to survive the seemingly unending onslaught from her patient, with (for a while) a two-hour supervision every week. But even the madness in this gradually became understandable, and the patient was slowly, and painfully, able to move on to a life that eventually began to flourish with creativity and professional success.

One thing that makes this book unusual is that (with the patient's permission and help) this clinical account is richly documented with extracts from the patient's own letters.

Another thing about this book is that it also illustrates and brings alive one of the most important, but difficult to understand, concepts of Winnicott: *the use of an object*. In this account the reader is able to see, and to experience, the impact of the attacks that had to be survived without collapse or retaliation, as Winnicott had described. Only thus was this patient able to discover a strength in her therapist that she could then rely on and use. Hitherto it had seemed that her therapist had only survived as a result of the patient's protecting her from everything in her mind that she had assumed no-one would survive – unless protected from all of that by her. It was only through this extraordinary sequence, so well documented in this book, that the patient described came to the healing that had never been possible before, however much re-parenting she had been given.

This carefully reported therapy can teach all of us much about the therapeutic process, its limitations and its potential.

Introduction

This is the story of a breakdown waiting to happen, the therapy and finally the recovery. The recovery can be described as life changing and transformative. The patient came, looking for a therapeutic experience which would fulfil a myth that claims: 'It is never too late to have a happy childhood'. Although the work began from this premise, in fact it was not the 'happy childhood' or reclaimed childhood that she discovered, but rather a path through the vicissitudes of her unhappy childhood. The therapy led to her life and relational world being transformed, from desperately unhappy to deeply creative, rich and satisfying.

The work was unusual in several ways. It cut across a number of different approaches to therapy and involved a unique and interesting set of circumstances. Resting on an integration of theories and methods, it nonetheless leaves certain questions still unanswered about some of the accepted understanding of what the critical factors are which lead to a 'cure' in a talking cure.

This account introduces the reader to the uncommon extent to which letters were written, received and allowed, from patient to therapist. These letters proved to be a gift to the work from both the patient's and the therapist's perspectives. The letters, extracts of which are reproduced here with the patient's permission, convey more powerfully than I can the impact of being with, and facing with the patient, the terrors in her mind. They show the urgency that developed within her to get the terror expressed, and to get rid of it by physically and concretely conveying her internal monsters to someone who could receive, listen to and process the feelings generated.

Thus the story ultimately reinforces an approach to therapy that rests on following the patient and her process, rather than leading it from a theoretical position. The work began with the seductive idea, mutually shared by the patient and therapist, that childhood deficit could be dealt with by creating the 'better parenting experience' in the present, following a so-called 're-parenting' model in order to find an assumed transformational experience. But this process can very quickly become addictive, thus failing for the same reasons that all addictive processes fail. They are ultimately not able to provide the longed for experience or meet, in this case, early unmet relational needs that appeared to be elusively just out of reach. This resulted in ever increasing demands to fulfil the phantasy – that more of the emotionally gratifying experience was what was needed to cure the childhood deficits. At the same time, the gratifying relationship protected both therapist and patient from exposure to the unimaginable horrors in childhood that arise for a neglected and abused child.

The escalating and ongoing demands reached a crisis point, which compelled me to search for a different way of working. In the first place, I was forced to wonder and question whether it was possible to find an alternate route. By relentlessly pushing for what she thought she needed, this patient (Jane) created an ever increasing tension and conflict between us. Another approach was needed, both conceptually and practically.

It was thus extremely fortunate that, in recognising the need for help, I met Patrick Casement who saw what was needed and, in becoming the supervisor of this case, was able to provide me with the necessary support, as well as the understanding, to carry the case forward to its successful outcome. Changing my way of being with this patient resulted in increasing her distress, which was originally about separation and abandonment. Now it was focused on my changing approach. Counter-intuitively I had stepped back from being the 'better mother', instead putting firm boundaries in place, but at the same time I remained in touch with the patient's distress and her feelings of rage and fear.

Naturally the patient initially escalated her demands, kept up the pressure, and spent a good deal of time and energy trying to convince me that my changing direction had been a mistake. As a consequence of this work, it became clear to me that the 'good experience' needed is ultimately provided in psychotherapy by finding someone who is willing to engage in the struggle, and able to respond to the patient's distress even when the therapist is perceived as the cause of the distress.

In the evolving direction of the therapy, what the supervision was also providing was a clear indication of the necessity for me to follow the patient's lead and listen to the clues, rather than having answers and 'knowing' what was needed, which a re-parenting model seems to encompass. In essence I had needed to find a way in which Jane could stop protecting me. She had been keeping me 'good', and keeping her own sense of badness away from our relationship, whilst continuing to feel herself to be the source of any evil or bad.

This mental shift, concerning the nature of the 'good experience' in therapy, cleared the way and made it possible for me to engage with what had seemed impossible for the patient to imagine could be heard and understood by another. Thus she was able to find the experience of being with someone who was willing to tolerate the horrors of her internal monsters, where it had in the past seemed as if there wasn't anyone capable or willing to do so in the past. The patient had constantly felt the need to protect the other from the imagined worst in herself. Through her therapist's not collapsing, retaliating or withdrawing, the patient came to experience that she and her therapist could survive the infantile and real horrors, and monsters in her phantasy. This led to an experience that had previously seemed an impossibility to her.

The structure of the book will be to take the reader into the experience by telling the story, describing aspects of the letters, and then we can follow the main clinical aspects of the work: namely the various features of the transference, the use of other modalities such as art therapy, the impact of supervision, the ending of the work and finishing with some clinical reflections and theoretical notions relating to the work.

Chapter 1

A search for a safe pair of hands

This chapter will introduce the story of the therapy, the central features in the patient/therapist dyad and the theoretical frame within which the work was embedded.

Setting the scene

This is the story of a breakdown and recovery. It is also the story of a therapy conducted over a period of seven years. It is described from a number of different perspectives with an interplay of internal and outer worlds and the space between them.

The patient's story

My version of the story of the therapy

It is a rare privilege to work with such a gifted patient as the person to be described in this book. She is gifted in her ability to use therapy, her commitment to the work, and her ability to capture her internal experience in words.

There have been numerous challenges in this work. In the first place, doing the therapy was challenging. At the completion of this therapy, however, I was faced with the challenge of describing the work. What makes the description so complex are the many parts to the story and the challenge of presenting them in a coherent and sequential fashion. Furthermore, in doing justice to the experience, there were other considerations such as the patient's wish that the emotional quality be preserved in some way. Thus I have included her words, where possible, as they particularly convey and capture something of the quality and flavour of the work. I have her words available to me in several ways:

from an interview we recorded some time after the therapy had ended; from various e-mails before, during and after; and some verbatim statements captured from the sessions; and, centrally, from the letters that were written to me throughout the entire duration of the work.

Including Jane in this way seems only appropriate and right in the spirit of our co-created work. It has been her consistent wish that, if there is value to others that can arise from this work, it be used as such. In that spirit I proceed, while at the same time being aware of the possibility of this interfering in some way with the anonymity, and confidentiality of the work.

As author, this presentation as a whole rests upon my own subjectivity, apart from the occasions when I can quote the patient verbatim. Even here my subjectivity is reflected in my choice of quotes. Thus there are numerous aspects to be thought about, including my story, the story of the work, the patient's story, the perspective from supervision and finally, but equally important to me, the theoretical implications that can be drawn from a rich and complex piece of work such as this. I have woven these elements together in order to create a coherent picture of the complex and multi-dimensional process that intense, individual, relationally oriented therapy can generate.

Jane's thoughts in this regard are:

> As far as protecting myself is concerned, obviously I would not want my name used. That would be more to protect me with people who don't already know because there are obviously those who lived with me through that time....

In another communication she added:

> I have also been thinking about the possible book. I want to have parts of the letters as part of that – and because of that I want a pseudonym – a bit like the letters themselves this allows a freedom which I could not allow – partly for my own protection. I am not interested in any kudos of co-authoring; more important to have the freedom to be real – particularly as I think this is one of the things which may help.

She continued with:

> In a way it's not about me anymore. It doesn't feel as if it is about me, rather about a period in my life. It was an incredibly

important, life-changing event but I'm not defined by it in the way I probably was at one time. I don't need to be attached to it and I don't need to be recognised for it. I am interested in letting people know. I think it gives hope and encouragement. I was helped by various accounts of successful work while I was going through my own therapy.

This work is positioned within a relational frame. It is clearly an example of therapy that is integrative and developmental. It is also inter-subjective and a story of co-creation. It is my own need to wrap theory around it. However I will leave the theoretical reflections till later and get on with the story.

The aim in this chapter is to tell the story – describe the work – and to conceptualise it within a frame that makes sense.

I will begin at the beginning and I will be calling my patient Jane.

The story begins where the work ends, because this account starts with a taped meeting that my patient and I had, some two years after the therapy had ended, and we had then not met with each other at all for some time. Jane's words that are quoted in this part come largely from the transcribed tapes of our retrospective reflections, which culminated in some discussion concerning a possible book about her journey through therapy.

The story of Jane's therapy

The initial meeting before the work had clearly started

My first meeting with Jane was in a workshop that I ran as a visiting trainer. At the time I was still living in South Africa although I had begun the process of moving to the UK.

I saw Jane as a tall, thin, pale woman. What I noticed immediately were the deep black rings around her eyes. There was an intensity about her and she was noticeable in the quality of contact she made as well as what seemed, even then, to be the depth of her despair.

In her words, retrospectively, she said:

> I think I just knew that if I was going to have a life this was my opportunity to find a life because I really think that life can bring a chance. I have lived such a tortured inner world. I mean

I knew I could not go on ... and meeting you seemed like an opportunity that I had been waiting for.

At the end of the third and final day, Jane enquired very nervously if she could ask me something. It was the last thing in my mind when she asked if she could come into therapy with me, despite the fact that I was not yet living in the UK at the time. It seemed to me that she was determined to get my agreement about therapy and would not take 'No' for an answer. Thus, in spite of the fact that I was still travelling backwards and forwards, I agreed that, on my coming to settle in England, I would be happy to work with her as a patient in a long-term therapy.

There was a precedent to this arrangement in the TA community, in the sense that some visiting trainers had contracts and therapy clients overseas. It was a practice I was already both critical of, somewhat skeptical, and worried about. However, Jane persisted and insisted saying that she would wait for me to come back to the UK. Further, she wanted to see me whenever I was in the country, which at that time was every few months.

Jane had added:

I don't know what would have happened if for some reason you could not see me. I guess I would have survived and got myself together, but at the time it felt like life and death.

The next year and the start of the regular weekly therapy

The way in which the work began inevitably shaped and coloured the therapy. Here the work formally began after a long period of waiting and anticipation, filled with hope and dread for her. Many years later she wrote to me about how she had been led to believe that healing would come if only she could find the right person and be a 'good enough' client. She had been labelled 'avoidant' by some of her previous therapists and trainers. So we began the work with a sense of herself that the healing she was seeking was just out of her reach, but I seemed to embody the solution. I appeared to her to be part of the dominant culture and it looked as if I could offer the good experience that held the key to her cure.

Jane was participating in a workshop run by another visiting trainer and I attended the workshop, largely as an observer. I had worked previously with this trainer in a variety of ways over the years. At this stage, however, I was simply intending to observe and think about the work.

I didn't know that I had been cast in the role of 'saviour' by Jane. Neither was I clear about what role the internationally well-known trainer saw me in, in that workshop (whether as assistant, colleague, commentator?).

On the first morning however the trainer literally threw the patient into my arms, saying something about her longing and waiting for me to arrive. I imagined he had intuitively picked up something about her waiting for me and her desperation to begin the work.

A retrospective comment that Jane made was:

> Our work started before you were in the country so I had probably had a year or more of longing before you arrived which also contributed to my breaking down.

So began a long and challenging journey together, full of intense emotions and remarkable moments. A journey that was going to be life-changing for Jane and which would give me the opportunity to learn, understand, and grow in my capacity as a therapist as well, of course, as a person. In fact this work transformed my own understanding and practice as a therapist, supervisor and teacher of psychotherapy.

Jane spent the next five days, almost wordless, deeply regressed and very physically close to me in the workshop. At the time we didn't talk much about that experience between us or how this had shaped and contributed to the subsequent work.

In her words Jane acknowledged how important it was to the powerful early transference that she developed in relation to me.

> And yet that was all part of my connection to you and part of what helped me to tolerate how awful it had all become....

During the five-day workshop, Jane created an opportunity to access some of her hidden aggression and violence, in order to show me and I think to warn me, by requesting time and space to work with both the visiting trainer and her previous therapist as co-therapists.

The group usually identifies with the client/patient in these scenarios and the therapist or therapists work with the presenting issue(s). These scenes are often highly charged and emotional as they invite the client to regress and experience from the therapist a different form of response than the one they might have got from parents. It certainly evokes a cathartic reaction and, in the immediacy of this experience, provides relief and often new insights into the childhood situation as, needless to say, regressed clients access their early experiences. However from my point of view, as observer in this case, it seemed somewhat artificial and it didn't make much sense. So it took me a long time in the therapy to connect this display of inner violence to the good compliant and scared patient that I saw in my consulting room.

Jane chose to travel quite a long way to London to see me. She knew that she needed a regular time and a space that should be as safe as possible, somewhat removed from her familiar environment.

From the beginning Jane was clear about what she felt she needed, and I trusted her sense of this by going along with it whenever I could. For example a regular 50-minute session felt too short and we always worked for a double session.

At the time I was working in a flexible way as I hadn't fully settled in London, or adjusted to my new working life, and I had not established a regular working schedule. However, I made sure to see Jane at the same time and same day each week. Thus, as the work proceeded it was contained within a regular weekly therapy session.

As I reflect on this unorthodox and somewhat shaky start, and wonder about its impact with the hindsight and understanding that I now feel I have, it seems to be related to how I thought about the work then. In this sense it carries the influence of working for years in the relatively disorganised and somewhat chaotic situation at the time in the South African context.

Here is an example of how today I might never have agreed to work in this fashion.

Jane retrospectively echoed my sentiments, saying:

> It's not the way I work here. It's not the way I work at all. And I can feel sniffy about people who do. I sometimes catch myself because I am feeling quite sniffy about people who work in this way. Maybe it's partly my experience of breaking down and what it means. I don't think I could have made the

transformation without breaking down, but whether it had to be so painful for so long I don't know either.

Jane and I were also commenting on how we had become increasingly critical of, and had strong reservations about, the practice of swooping into a group, making powerful interventions and then departing again having often generated therapeutic crises, and leaving much of the necessary sustained hard work of the therapeutic containment to others.

So, despite these reservations, there was clearly something powerful and valuable in engaging in a process that felt possible, and working it out from there. She was a patient looking for a therapist and I was a therapist available to work with a patient.

By the time we began working Jane was by no means a naïve patient, having already had much therapy and also having completed several trainings in psychotherapy. She was already practising as a therapist, engaged in supervision, and was well regarded by colleagues and supervisors. This background will become evident, as we see how she was able to reflect upon, comment on and contribute greatly to, this body of work through her insight, capacity for self-reflection and knowledge of the field, and her general level of skill. At the same time all who met her professionally, in whatever capacity, could recognise her distress.

At the beginning of the work I was equally not a naïve therapist. However, I took Jane's initial presentation at face value and was completely unprepared for the regression and collapse that followed, as we began to engage more regularly. Nevertheless, throughout the strenuous process of the therapy, Jane continued to function, held down a job, looked after her children and home, and even managed from time to time to lighten up and have a bit of fun. Generally though, I would have described her at the time as being anxious and deeply depressed, on the edge of a psychotic depression for a number of years before and during the early to middle stages of the work.

Jane said of this:

> On one level I could do that, I could act appropriately but it had no bearing on what I was experiencing on the inside. I mean I could be completely regressed and talk forever as, in a way, I'd done that all my life. I also knew I had to take the fear somewhere and I thought,

> when I watched you in that workshop, that my hope was you would have the understanding of what the chaos was about. You would not simply want me to put a lid on it. Maybe that's what I had always been told: 'Put a lid on it, you have a choice to put a lid on.' That was abusive but not intentionally so.

In the early stages of the work, I was doing what I was used to doing as a therapist. By this time I had been working as a therapist for some fifteen years and, prior to my formal training in South Africa, as a psychotherapist engaged in various 'people related' work such as counselling, crisis work, interviewing, and teaching psychology at a university.

My frame for understanding the work at that stage was primarily a humanistic one, based on an integration of Transactional Analysis with Gestalt Therapy, a TA/Gestalt approach that was influenced by Developmental Psychology, which I taught as an academic discipline, and some superficial understanding of Self Psychology and Object Relations theory gained largely from reading.

At the time I was impressed by the value and the power of what could be described as negotiated regression. I had seen how feelings from the past could be accessed therapeutically, by those active approaches to therapy, and integrated into the present adult functioning to good effect. I was however completely unprepared for the instantaneous and persistent regression that happened as Jane and I began to work.

Of this Jane commented:

> At some level I started going into regression in workshops years before meeting you. I knew that's what I needed. In some way, though, I kept getting kicked (blamed) quite a bit because when I was regressed I wasn't easy to control, and what wasn't available to me was sufficient 'adult' self to be appropriate. So they weren't very pleasant experiences. Some of them were, however, very important because I think they put me in touch with all that stuff that came out later in our work, and in the art therapy. I became aware of a part of myself that I hadn't really contacted before.

Jane is describing here the pain of having to appear sane and the pressure to manage herself.

However I wasn't asking her to put a lid on, as I was used to working with high levels of affect as a result of the training and experience in that kind of work and because of seeing so many traumatised people. Thus a person's need to express intense feelings in sessions was something I was comfortable with. At that early stage, however, I was not fully in touch with Jane's level of distress and how primitive some of her experience was. It was during the separations and breaks in the work that I became aware of the depth of her regression, and how frightened and distressed she was.

Here Jane's words were:

> It is really interesting how, in a sense, what attracted me into the work with you was the re-parenting therapy and of course, if you remember, before we ever really started work together there was that five-day workshop ... In a sense I'd been prepared for that by all the training I'd done, because the training focused on that, so I was becoming more and more permanently regressed really. And in my mind the only way through it was to contract, in a way, to be in that state. But it just happened I had no control over it. Having said that, it felt as though it had been waiting to happen all my life and that's what I was searching for. I had had ten years of therapy by then, which was very, very helpful in holding me and bringing up my children. But it just did not address the core issues, which is what the regression seemed to tie up with, and I don't know if we would have had this outcome if it had not been for that, you see ...

Re-parenting, from the perspective of Transactional Analysis, is an approach to psychotherapy that invites the regressed patient into the role of the child while the therapist moves into a role of being the better parent, known as the 'nurturing parent', rather than a critical, neglectful, abusive or failing parent, which was probably what the patient's experience had been in childhood. It could be seen as a form of 'role playing', although it often had the quality of authenticity with a patient slipping into, for example, a 'home language' which may be an early one used in childhood.

Jane continued:

> I think I've been containing it for years. I think I've been containing it since I had children really, but probably before that

too. Particularly, the pressure for me having children put me beyond my capacity. I think I had always coped reasonably well. I managed one child OK but two was beyond my capacity.

So, I was listening, reflecting back what I was hearing and, I think, being fairly directive – even prescriptive. Certainly, I was being placed into the 'parent' role but I was getting into this more unconsciously than in my full awareness. I was guided in my mind by ideas of re-parenting, being the better parent and providing the 'emotionally corrective experience', as was Jane. She very clearly, from the beginning, saw me as her 'real' mother: the mother she didn't have, the better mother, the 'if only *she* had been my mother my life would have been different' therapist.

I remember feeling more and more stressed and strained and a bit desperate at times. I tried a variety of techniques. For example, I did a number of 'Parent Interviews'. This is a technique TA therapists used to use at the time, inviting or asking their clients to 'pretend', imagine or role play, being one of the client's own parents. At those times she gave me the sense and experience of the vicious and mad mother who had raised her, based on her early relationship with her mother, I believe.

Jane said of this:

> I also think our work started before you were in the country, so I had probably a year or more of longing before you arrived, which also contributed to the breakdown.

Some of the pertinent biographical details are as follows. My patient was the second child in a family of four children. She had an older brother and a younger sister, and the youngest was another brother. She and the younger brother, whom she looked after and protected to the best of her ability, were in an alliance to deal with the family situation differently to the other two. The younger sister and the older brother adopted an anti-social defence against the pathology in the family, anti-social to the extent that they were both in serious trouble in the external world and acted out their pain with a good deal of real violence and destruction to themselves and others.

Jane's description of this:

> But the public would have seen four all nicely turned out, well dressed children. I remember the neighbours saying, they're a proud family.

In the early stages of the work Jane's relationship with her sister came in and out of the discussions. She was seriously afraid that her sister wanted to kill her. Although there was a fair degree of paranoia in this worry there was also a strong element of psychological truth to her anxiety.

Jane's father had been dead for a number of years, and during the course of the therapy her elderly mother got sick and died. Later in the work her younger sister also died as result of illness, caused I think largely by the abuse of serious drugs. Her sister had also been in trouble with the law on drug-related charges.

In the earlier stages of our work, however, Jane was still visiting and looking after her by now aging and physically deteriorating mother. Of course, in the therapy we were dealing with the mother in the patient's mind and memory from the past, who had little to do with the real old lady – her mother of the present time or the mother the neighbours would have described.

The details are vaguer now but Jane's maternal grandmother had not only been somewhat mentally disturbed but she also seems to have been sadistic and cruel. This family, who were country folk, were known in their community to be cruel to their animals – hard and difficult. The patient's own mother, to the neighbours and the outside world, was known as a respectable and 'nice' lady. She was, however, also described as 'odd'.

Another therapist, friend and colleague of the patient who knew her socially, once said to me that the mother was probably 'multiple' – some sort of dissociative personality disorder. In a way similar to her daughter, however, she (the mother) displayed a veneer of normality as a nurse and midwife.

One of the stories my patient Jane told me about her mother's early experience was that she, the mother (the youngest in her family) remembered her own mother (Jane's grandmother) starting to sing hymns before she became particularly violent and cruel to her children.

The cruelty and neglect in the patient's own childhood experience appears to have been largely psychological. It could have been direct assaults on her sense of being. She seems to have been a scapegoat for the mother, usually treated with scorn and derision. She described being dragged along, being looked at with disgust and sneering, by her mother, thus experiencing continuous attacks on her sense of self.

Jane's younger sister had serious eczema as a young baby and child, demanding a good deal of the mother's attention. Both she and the older brother were described as very aggressive, thus dealing with the family and the difficulties in the family in a very different way to Jane who is inherently sensitive, having a gentle and caring nature that made her vulnerable and unable to defend herself from emotional assaults. She was closest in her family to her youngest brother, protecting and looking after him from a young age. The father seems to have been emotionally absent and unable to help the children in any psychological way.

The first crisis

As the days of the first year of our work together drew to a close and the days got shorter, darker and colder, I prepared for what was to become my annual return to South Africa, during the Christmas and early January holiday. In many ways, this was the worst time of the year for a longish break of several weeks in therapy, since it was mid-winter and an unusual time for a therapist to take a break, unlike in the summer. We discussed the coming break in our work. It was clearly going to be very difficult for her to deal with a separation then, some six months into the regular weekly therapy, as she was in a full-blown regression and in a very dependent transference in relation to me.

It was agreed that Jane's previous therapist, someone she had worked with before our work commenced, would see her while I was away. This was to prove to be an unsatisfactory arrangement but then neither were the subsequent substitutes that we later tried.

Any 'locum' therapist who looks after a patient, particularly a regressed and vulnerable one, is put into a 'baby sitting' role, which is neither satisfying nor comfortable.

Somehow Jane managed that first winter break, although she was very distressed. There were some sporadic phone calls and, more importantly, that was when Jane's letters really began. Both of these (phone calls and letters) were to prove to be significant contacts and an important aspect of the work.

Jane later said of that early phase:

> I mean, looking back, I had a major breakdown. How I kept walking and working I will never know. I had a breakdown that lasted several years.

The second year

Residential conference

At the beginning of the second year, soon after we resumed our regular weekly sessions, I was to be on the staff of a residential conference in Europe. The format of the conference, which was called 'Script and Group Process', was a week-long residential programme comprising the following: every day there was a slot for small group work, which was conducted as a therapy group; in addition, there were other processes which involved participants and staff, including a large group, inter-groups and theory slots.

As I was therapist to one of the small groups I thought that, if Jane wanted to come as a participant, it would give us a chance to work every day for a week and provide some frame for intensive contact.

I was still thinking in the earlier mode of how the work had begun the previous summer, with a five-day intensive residential – naïvely, so it turned out. It proved to be an extremely stressful and painful experience for Jane, she having to share me and my attention, and being exposed to my relating to others. In retrospect this was not a procedure to recommend. Yet, it did help in the building of experience between us – including, of course, my willingness to try and think of creative opportunities of working together.

As we spoke about this early incident I said, 'Maybe if we had been able to put something into words.' And she responded with:

> I think it still would have been in some way intolerable. It's really strange when I think back on those sessions. I mean, I gained something from the whole experience. It was just incredible to be there with all those people doing what you do and yet ... as a matter of fact, I made a good contact with people ... even though I wasn't realistic then – but I thought somehow you would be mine when I was there and of course I was shocked to find I had to share you with the whole conference. I was very brave and it was a great demand on me to keep on track, switching worlds.

This experience underlines, among other things, that there is no way of hurrying up or condensing developmental work of this nature. At this stage, though, I was still firmly into a re-parenting and replacement conceptualisation of therapy. From that perspective I saw the course as an opportunity for bounded, intense, daily contact. At the same time I was missing the other implications of this.

On reflection, the change of role and the disruption to the process of therapy could only be described in the mildest way as confusing and in the more extreme sense as disturbing and traumatic. It was obvious to me, quite quickly, that I could not provide the necessary containment or concentrate on Jane when I was engaged in another task – in spite of the way I had seen some visiting international experts engaged with a number of regressed patients at the same time in workshops.

We continued through a second year of regular therapy with some short breaks, each of which were difficult for the patient. After the experience at the residential conference in Europe I decided it was too complicated and painful for Jane to attend such public situations, like my workshops or seminars. We had a few tussles about this but in the end she avoided, wherever possible, seeing me in a public forum.

Jane commented on that experience by describing how bad she felt about herself because of the intense feelings of envy and possessiveness that such situations evoked in her:

> I've never really gone for people that I have wanted. I think, looking back on it, that my fear was I would become obsessively jealous and it would be intolerable every time I met with the other people ... of course that was going on every time I saw you in public, conferences etc., but what was intolerable was being in the world and being this evil.

An initial reflection on the letters and how they became a unique contribution to the work

I am introducing the letters, and their place in the work, now because they formed such a central feature that I will return to in more detail – using extracts from them to highlight Jane's and my developing understanding of their significance. This present section is simply to locate them in the overall narrative.

Well into the second year the letters became firmly established. The letters will be described in a separate section (Chapter 6) as they form a particular and valuable insight into the work and the process of Jane's therapy. For now it is sufficient to say a few introductory things.

The regular writing to me had begun during my absences overseas, as a way of maintaining contact with me and keeping herself in my mind. It was only when, during this time, she started writing almost daily that I realised the letters had become a regular feature of the therapy.

The letters then posed some dilemmas for me since they were in many ways an essential feature of our work together and yet they were beyond the boundaries of the therapeutic space.

The dilemmas were both practical and conceptual: how to use them and what they meant were to be ongoing problems for me. I always recognised that they were playing a significant and valuable role in the work. It is only now, in retrospect, that I can fully appreciate how helpful they proved to be.

We hear from the patient's point of view how central the letters were in keeping her functioning, and they partly explain how she managed the internal distress and state of breakdown while appearing to be coping with her external world. She described aspects of her internal world and the split between what people see on the outside and her inner experience.

In our retrospective conversation she said, talking about the re-parenting model:

> Here I think that's where the limitation of the theory of that model comes in because I think they were working on a model in which people always have access to an adult self.

I said: 'that's what you were told'.

> Absolutely. On one level I could do that so I could act appropriately, but it had no bearing on what I was experiencing on the inside. I mean, I could be completely regressed and talk forever in a way that I'd done all my life and, in a way, what that level of therapy did was simply reinforce all that, because it was the adult talking which was acceptable while, actually, the internal chaos was effectively hidden ... I knew I had to have somewhere to take the fear. I think, when I watched you in lectures, my hope was that you would have the understanding of what the chaos was about. You would not simply want me to put a lid on it.

We see here how the letters were part of this desperate attempt to communicate something, which she couldn't do in conversation, and have it understood.

The fact that, through the letters, Jane was able to put her feelings into words, rather being expressed through cutting, vomiting, self-harming etc. – albeit at times into primitive language – was very important and eased the stress and anxiety for me about her state of functioning and potential for far more distressing acting out. Further it had to do with expression, communication and understanding.

Perhaps the most central aspect of all, in relation to the letters, was the direct window they provided into her inner state – as well as the way they carried the unconscious thread between us – and the continuity between the current process and the past.

In some ways this became a unique example of a relationship that was completely real while at the same time a phantasy. The letters had the quality that all imaginative and creative processes have, in that they came from the inner world and also bridged internal and external realities. They provided an almost poetic view of a 'troubled mind' as well as an able, brave and extraordinarily psychologically gifted subject.

Jane said of this:

> And of course the letters come to mind because they could argue in a way a continuous thread that became the conversation we would have had, or probably would not have had because I would not have said those things.

Another function of the letters, to the story of the therapy, was the way they changed in quality and content, indicating the progress and process of the work.

As Jane remembered years after the work was complete:

> It felt like a relief to me, to write the letters. I wrote the letters because I had to, almost, as if I didn't choose to. I had to in order to stay sane, so they were absolutely a way of keeping myself functioning because the internal pressure was so hard. That was what the letters did. It was a way to keep the internal pressure at a manageable level.

The writing escalated from a letter or two while I was away to every few days until there would be a number arriving on the same day, both when I was overseas and when we were meeting regularly in London.

> When I wrote more than one, because I would write a letter and experience some relief once it was in the box ... and yet on

some days the pressure would be very high again and I would have to write another one. I think it took the place of what some people would do with cutting, actually.

Here we get a clue as to some of the importance of the letters to the therapy. It was the patient's own reflections which were so seminal in fully understanding some of these processes. Jane continued in this conversation as we spoke about what the letters meant to her:

> What I have experienced with them was almost a physiological surge. It then just poured out onto paper. Then I sent them to you and I could feel some relief. Sometimes there were several surges in one day.

And also:

> It was really important that we didn't talk about them too much because I think if you had tried to unpick them it would have limited me in writing, because I would have resented myself....

This was a clear statement as to how she feared becoming too self-conscious and therefore self-censoring and ashamed of the primitive, regressed and violent nature of the extremes in some of the letters.

In another conversation Jane had added, on reflection:

> I was thinking that one of the most important things for me was that you never asked me to account for the letters. If you had brought them to the sessions and asked me to talk about what was written then I would have had to stop writing, or the writing would have been 'thoughtful' and censored. Instead of being a vehicle for communicating the 'raw material' of my pain.

She continued with another thought, equally relevant:

> The other thing was that you could appreciate my 'insanity' and my 'sanity' at the same time – that both were true concurrently. I spent most of my life living out my 'sanity' with the tremendous internal pressure of madness. With you there was the space to

be mad without having to sacrifice my sanity. Even at my worst I knew that I would never let go of my sanity. If a choice had to be made – it would be the choice to be sane – but that would have been a terrible price to pay. I now live without the pressure of madness because you allowed me to be fully mad in the letters – and in the paintings.

Summing up, I could say that the letters were a 'tale of a breakdown'. They also held the madness that she was so clearly in touch with.

The end of the second year

As we approached the winter break in the second year, we again discussed the problem of my absence and how we could bridge it. Being the creative and resourceful person that she was, even while very ill, Jane suggested she work with someone in London, completely out of the humanistic network.

I, by now, was well aware of how difficult the break was for Jane. Further, neither phoning nor writing had made it any easier. In fact, if anything, the experience of phone calls to South Africa had been particularly distressing, as she describes here:

> When I think of the early days, when I used to phone you from call boxes before we had arranged about the phoning, if you see what I mean, I'd just have this big bag of pound coins to pile into phone boxes often – you know what phone boxes were like – smelly, littered walls all those things, in a way that all highlighted the difference between us. It's almost like the external environment was my internal environment, and then my imagining your sunshine and beaches and nice house. All of those things underlined my internal experience and the difference between us.

The problem with phone calls

Since my winter break was longer than usual, as I would return to South Africa for about five weeks over Christmas, Jane graphically described the problem with phoning as an attempt to bridge some of the gap created in the work by my absence.

> Because, actually, even though we had an agreement that I could phone, of course I would often phone and someone else

would answer the phone or you wouldn't be there, or I'd have to ring tomorrow or I'd ring and you'd gone out. I'd just build up the courage to make the phone call and also the humiliation. I felt incredibly humiliated that I would need to have to keep doing this, and yet I couldn't not do it. So that was what was very hard. I think I kind of became obsessive, and thinking about you, imagining what you were doing and thinking I would bring my sleeping bag to your doorstep; all kinds of things, in themselves very humiliating – to have those thoughts is actually very humiliating

She added however:

It was much better after we'd had a time arranged for phone calls.

I was helped with this problem by my new supervisor, Patrick Casement, who proved to be so instrumental to the change in the work. In this case he explained how potentially unhelpful it could be, to say to a patient you can call if you need to. This can create for the therapist a view of themselves as generous and helpful, which may alleviate their guilt. However it can make it difficult and painful for the patient, who can find themselves unable to express their anger in the face of needing to be grateful for the therapist's generosity. At the time she was unable to describe the painful process she went through before making any call to me.

When phone sessions become properly negotiated, as paid-for sessions, it can be freeing for both patient and therapist. The therapist does not feel they are being so generous and helpful, with all the potential for becoming resentful and acting out a sense of imposition, intrusion or ingratitude. Likewise, the patient may be freed from some of the pain described here and freed up to express more of their natural upset, anger and distress at the therapist's absence.

In the second break

I recommended a Jungian Analyst, as a 'holding therapist'. Although I didn't know her personally, she came highly recommended by a colleague. At the time I was hopeful that this would be productive and useful.

In retrospect, although there may have been some value in this experience, on balance Jane's journeys to London in the dark of winter, only to deal with the pain of the abandonment, sounded to me (on my return) awful and not particularly holding or supportive. As I reflect on this further, I think it was better than I had felt it to be, because at least something of her inner reality was being attended to, painful as it was.

The third year

And so a second year of work went by and the third year began. At some point during this year two things happened.

I was by now feeling badly stuck and wondering, questioning the value of going through another painful and difficult break in the work, and whether this was either productive or in fact even viable.

Jane made an important point about the limitation of the model we were both using at the time. She was able to see very clearly at this stage that there was no way in which there was a possibility of meeting her archaic need and yearning within the context of a psychotherapy relationship.

> I'm just thinking about a lot of things. Part of it was that I don't think either of us was wanting to do it, and I think it was because we were between models, and the humanistic model actually does not address what was happening at all. And I think that is where previously I had ended up, feeling more damaged because what I was experiencing was simply nothing to do with how it was understood, and I began to blame myself.
>
> At that point it felt like nothing would have helped bar you kind of adopting me and helping me move in, and even then it would not have been enough.

She was reflecting these thoughts about our work while I had fortuitously met Patrick Casement and he agreed to take on the supervision of this therapy. He is of course a psychoanalyst and approached the work from that frame. The patient was not consciously aware of the change in supervisors and how rapidly I was being affected by the new understanding I was getting from Patrick Casement.

There is much to be said about this experience and the impact of that new supervision on the work. I will therefore return (later) to talking in more detail about the place of supervision and this particular supervision to the work. For now I want to express my gratitude and appreciation for the flexibility and open-mindedness with which Patrick approached the work.

As I had never taped any of the work with Jane, I would bring to supervision the *verbatim* accounts of the session which I could capture after the session finished. Although not as accurate an account as recordings would be, these remembered sessional notes of course represented my subjectivity in the process. We discussed the sessions in terms of the way in which the patient might be experiencing what I was saying and doing. What was extraordinarily powerful, from the beginning, was how this process put me in touch with my own unconscious communication and what I might be relaying to the patient through what I was doing and saying.

As I have already said, at this stage I was still working actively and very hard at being a good mother, the 'better parent', while at the same time feeling more and more stuck and despairing and probably angry. The sessions had also become ritualised with the patient regressing probably before she even arrived, curling up on the couch, often sucking her thumb and insisting on being looked after like a small child. Among other things I was feeling very controlled by her, and I had even agreed to sit with her on the couch.

I was doing things like reading young children's stories to her and drawing. I think the limit was reached in my supervisor's eyes when, in an attempt to try even harder, I had baked some cookies and we iced them in the session. At the time, I remember his expression said something like 'Did you really do that?' Years later, when he looked back on his early notes from that time, he confirmed that he had in fact written a question mark – indicating something like 'she didn't really do that did she?'

Jane said:

> Because there is something about the engagement. That the power of the engagement which I don't know would have been there had we not worked in that way. If we had only worked, with you sitting at the other end of the room and us talking about what it was like, my guess is that I would have stayed very cognitive.
>
> As I say, I still think that during that time when we were working in that (earlier) way I had internalised you, and that

experience mitigated the awfulness of the time when I became both terrified and furious with you. It's not just talking about the absence of it but providing something concrete that was actually very helpful. What I'm thinking is that the work can't be done, alone?

The early part of the work, which could be thought of as the 're-parenting' relationship, started from the beginning and ran through until the third year. It was changing as, although I was trying harder and harder, Jane appeared not to be getting any better. On the contrary, she was still wishing for more and yet would always leave sessions with a sense of longing and yearning. That way of working during that time had become a shared perspective as I didn't have another way to think about long-term therapy with a regressed and dependent patient.

It will be important to come back to these statements by the patient and think about them more explicitly in terms of the overall results of the work.

Suffice now to say that her view can be seen as supporting an Integrative Approach within which the early work in some therapies would be to create and provide a positive platform from which to hold the vicissitudes of the necessary negatives, which need to find a place for expression within the therapy. What is being raised here is one of the questions that this work asks and I will deal with this explicitly in the final chapters.

The theoretical and containing support from this new supervision that I was experiencing in the third year now began to give me hope. This was particularly so as I could see that my supervisor was both interested and challenged by the work. Patrick somehow communicated to me that he saw the possibility of continuing this work towards a positive outcome, even though it was only a few hours a week, and it became possible to contain difficult breaks in the therapy.

The art therapy

As we came up to the third break in the work, Jane had a new idea for bridging my absence. In contrast to the dark and dreary time of the previous winter, she thought that art therapy would be a useful and a creative option. Neither she nor I, from our shared humanistic perspective, accounted for the impact of blank paper, and the potential that created to access the unconscious, or for that method to trigger or expose the psychotic features in Jane's inner world.

The first indication I had that the art therapy was not providing the relief or support we had hoped for was when I received a phone call in South Africa from a rather upset and anxious art therapist.

Jane's words on this:

> I think you, and in fact both of us, didn't understand about the space ... I mean the experience of the art for me. The experience of the art therapy for me was ... I was stunned by what happened in the art ... It really surprised me ... The difficulty was she knew ... because she kept wanting me ... in a way she didn't understand what her function was. She started to get annoyed that I was keeping her out. I actually did not want her in. This wasn't about her at all. She was providing the space and the containment and material, and all of that, but actually this was about my relationship with you. I think she got very pissed off. I don't know how that figured with her way of looking at things or what she thought this was about ... so it sounds a bit like she was saying what about me, me, me.

To be fair to the art therapist, I think she got scared about the level of Jane's distress and was concerned that she was going to have a breakdown while I was away.

However Jane says:

> Interesting, I wasn't in the least scared. Although there was the experience of the art which allowed something to be put onto the paper. It felt a bit like writing a letter ... it was just that something got pulled onto the paper. It was not frightening to me at all. I never had any sense that I was out of control, or likely to be out of control, or that I was going crazy. I experienced it as a kind of another part of me, but there was never a sense that I was losing it. If anything it kept me sane.

When reflecting on her subjective experience of her art therapy, Jane appeared to be managing her external life (without hospitalisation or decompensating in her real world) and it made sense to me that she wasn't particularly anxious about the psychotic material that was surfacing. She had long been in touch with that side of herself.

I said to her: 'I was in touch with you so I wasn't unduly worried about you. I just remember my initial fears. But I also felt it was my fault I since left the art therapist to baby sit. I had wanted her to just hold the space for you to use.'

She said:

> She was almost offended that you kicked her out.

I said: 'It seems as if it felt like you were needing to reassure her.'
She carried on:

> But in a way she wasn't doing her job well enough. I wasn't interested in having a relationship with her. I mean it was fine for her to be there but I wasn't interested in being in a relationship with her.

To be fair to the art therapist, neither of us (Jane and I) knew clearly what we were doing or what we really expected or wanted from the art therapy, so the confusion was understandable.

Further describing the experience of doing the art Jane said:

> I am just remembering what it was like. I would choose the material or whatever I wanted. There would be a blank piece of paper. I would sit for a while, then I would actually experience a physiological change. I just can't explain it more than that. I would experience a physiological change and this stuff would pour out. I was just in it, but it was important for me to allow it. The other thing that pissed me off was when she kept trying to put a frame around it. It felt like she was trying to contain me. But I didn't want her frame. I didn't need it, but of course she didn't know that I could actually contain myself.
>
> I knew from you that I wasn't damaged. I mean all she had to do was provide the material and the presence. It was important that she had a presence. That there was a witness.
>
> Also, what she didn't know was that I have got enough control not to do it [go mad or commit suicide?]. Because I knew that I would never do it. I could allow myself to think about it, imagine it, and experience it. In a way it's weird that I don't have to.

I mean I've worked with people who have acted those things out, and that was the difference between me and them really.

I guess I understand the compulsion. I feel grateful that I didn't have to act those things out. I didn't have to put up with the further humiliation of everybody knowing. It was a secret, you were in on the secret (through the letters as well as the therapy).

Most importantly I didn't want her (the art therapist's) interpretations. All I wanted was a sort of 'Hello, how are you' kind of thing. But I didn't want to be told what it meant. I didn't mind being asked: I didn't want to be told. And I didn't want to be stopped, which made me realise that she had got frightened and tried to stop me. I wasn't psychotic. I was completely sane, yet there was this really primitive part which was always being pushed down.

I said: 'You were obviously searching for something beyond words ... for something to be released...'.

Actually, doing them (the paintings) was completely charged: talking about them wasn't. It released a different part of me. I didn't want her to stop me. It made me realise she was frightened when she tried to stop me: that I would become psychotic. But I wasn't psychotic. I was completely sane; and, yes, there was this real primitive part which was always being pushed down.

This conversation about the art therapy, years later, clarified much of what had gone on and what had distressed the art therapist so much. At the time, neither of them voiced the anxiety about psychosis to me. When Jane brought some of the pictures to show me, on my return, it then became glaringly apparent that the challenge for me was how to bring the process of what had happened in the art therapy into our sessions.

In talking about the letters and the art therapy, Jane said:

I think that there were a number of things. The paintings were a relief. There was a way in which they kept me sane. The huge relief was, it was a bit like the painting was. It was just like vomiting, although vomiting is something you do when you are ill. It felt healthier than that in some way. It felt like getting something out that is poisonous. More like lancing an abscess or something like that.

Turning point

While considering the challenge of bringing the material from the art therapy into being expressed directly to me, a number of things happened. By now I was becoming well held in the psychoanalytic supervision and so my understanding of the work was beginning to change significantly. I was therefore becoming able to think more explicitly about the unconscious elements in Jane's communications, and what might be going on between us, as more than just the obvious (superficial) re-enactment of a parent/child dynamic.

As our conversation reached the critical point of considering how the change between us started to emerge, Jane reflected by repeating an earlier sentiment:

> I think we were between models, and the humanistic model actually does not address what was happening at all. Where previously I had ended up feeling more damaged because what I was experiencing was simply adding more blame to myself ...

Describing my own experience of tension, and the need for something to change quite radically, I was also feeling increasingly uncomfortable about the acting out of the re-parenting process in the sessions while at the same time still uncertain about how to proceed.

In an early session at the beginning of the fourth year I took the bull by the horns. Well supported by the supervision and my developing understanding, and with confidence from a different view of the work, I precipitated a crisis. I moved off the couch next to Jane and across the room to a separate chair.

She commented about her experience of this dramatic change, marked by my physical moving, soon after returning at the beginning of the fourth year:

> I think it must have been when you had gone away. You'd gone in one mode and came back in another. Of course it was a terrible shock and I guess the shocking thing was I didn't understand, because during your absence I had had no contact

with you. I guess in that sense it reminded me of my mother. She would just change and I had no clue what had caused the change. I felt punished. All the time you were away there was the longing for you to come back in the old way and of course when you came back you'd changed and I took it as a criticism of me.

As I reflect now on my sudden decision to move, I can see that we had created a powerful enactment: in that moment I had become the unpredictable mother. I also think that there was an unconscious push between us, as I moved during this session without having really thought it through as something planned or premeditated.

This dramatic move happened a few months after the supervision with Patrick Casement began. By that time I had understood what the conceptual problems with the 'better' mother approach were, and why this led to the sense in the therapy of something being both repetitive and stuck between us. At the same time I think there was an urgency from Jane, for her to be able to express directly to me some of the destructive and aggressive feelings she was experiencing in relation to me.[1]

At the point of my moving Jane, seemingly in a psychotic state, said in great distress 'I feel as if you are 10,000 miles away', and I suddenly felt as if at last we had her earlier experience expressed in the room between us. Now we had the experience in the room of what happened when I was in Africa. I was no longer hearing about it through phone calls, second hand from the art therapist or disguised in the distress of the letters to me. The situation had been re-created between us and it was now possible to work directly in that space together.

This move now initiated a new regime so to speak. From then on I always stayed across the room in a separate chair. We had a number of sessions stretching over some months during which she continued to feel strange and estranged, but also angry and able to express this directly to me – about my withdrawal from the physical proximity to her. As I stated, I became now much closer to her mind and to her experience of me as the withdrawing, dismissing and uncaring mother.

In describing her felt experience at this time, Jane said:

> What was interesting in this was a lot of the pain became actual physiological pain. I mean my body was in agony and that was terrible.

I remember how distressed and pained she was.
Jane carried on:

> It was absolutely terrible. It was at those times I could feel myself going. I mean being so tensed, experiencing physical pain and feeling completely destitute.

She went on to explain:

> I don't really have a strong memory of this except I suppose there was a loss of hope, because I believed that somehow you would make me better – unless you were going to stop doing that and then there would be no hope.

I distinctly remember Jane saying at about this time: 'You have to hold the hope.' I realised we were in some sort of crisis, but not how close she had come to giving up hope as she experienced my change of course. Given that, in her mind, the road to cure lay along a re-parenting route it must have been frightening on two levels: the therapist part of her suddenly worrying that I was no longer on the same page; the child part of her re-experiencing and feeling the loss.

In this phase, some months into the new regime, a number of things happened in the therapy. Jane would at times go to the bathroom where there was a large mirror. Somehow, feeling so distorted and gross, she needed physical proof that her features hadn't altered. At the same time she warned me that if she ran out of the room I should not attempt to restrain her, because that would cause her to fight back violently. We were now close to the violence that she had tried to demonstrate in that early workshop so long ago. Further, she did seem to lose hope for a while, and on a number of occasions begged me to hold the hope as she could not hold on to it herself.

Thus the therapy moved into a new phase with her distress being palpable. While things got much more difficult and painful between us, I also breathed a sigh of relief because I could now feel that we were getting unstuck.

There was still a long way to go and we were clearly not out of the woods. I did not have any idea then of how long the process would take, but I began to feel that a necessary change in the work was happening, both in the process and the content, thus something new was going to become possible for her and between us. During this time I was experiencing the important support of my supervisor, which made all the difference to me in navigating these then (for me) uncharted waters.

Jane's reflection about the changed therapeutic approach that had begun to create both a new, real and powerfully different, dynamic between us was:

> I think that what was right was that alone[2] would not have done the trick. I could not have tolerated the pain. Either I would simply not have contacted that aspect of myself, like I had not in any other therapy previously. I had a way of managing to stay intact and working in a sensible way. We had been re-looking at things in a way that essentially left me untouched. It would have helped me to cope better but still untouched. It was the experience of the regression that caused me to break down. I mean looking back I had a major breakdown. I kept walking and working while the breakdown lasted several years.

On the other hand, the long period of positive holding and re-enactment seemed to have created a platform from which to withstand the vicissitudes of what was now to come.

In many ways, my moving across the room precipitated her ability to be able to use me to represent the 'mad' and inconsistent mother. It was in working now directly with the negative transference in the room that I truly got to grips with the notion of the 'use of an object'. Until this time, that notion of Winnicott's was one I could only understand conceptually but I did not truly know how to work with it clinically.

The ending of the work, when we finally agreed that we had come to a good place to finish, came naturally and easily after all the battles and conflicts. There was something about both of us knowing that the work was complete.

Jane had resolved the difficulties in her previous marriage and was now with someone who was good to her and able to take care of and look after her from a mature, respectful and loving position. Her children were grown and had left home and she had completed her counselling training and was fully qualified. In terms of the Freudian criteria, she was indeed able 'to love and work' and able to live in the world in a creative and satisfying way.

The above has been a brief overview of the story of the therapy. It is based on a conversation we (Jane and I) had several years after the work was completed. Her words come verbatim from the taped transcript. This account shows the highlights of the work that stood out for both of us as we talked about it some years after the ending. Significantly also we did not meet in my consulting room but some distance from London and thus in a neutral place.

However, it is worth noting that something of the essence of the work, different to conversations reported above, is captured in the letters. They have immediacy, often being written immediately after sessions, and express the quality of the inner processing, debriefing and sharing of her inner experience. It is the letters, more than anything else, that introduce and provide the material from which to understand Jane's internal process. And they give a unique window into an internal world of a breakdown and the healing that a therapeutic relationship can provide. Thus I have chosen not only to include brief pieces but also to devote a chapter to consider, with her help, the function and place the letters had in the therapy.

But, before coming to the content which follows this outline in more detail, by describing the various elements and illustrating them from the different sources, it is necessary to introduce something about my subjectivity and influences: where I come from, in terms of understanding and clinical experience and the perspective of a two-person psychology with both subjectivities central to the work, its content, process and outcome.

Who am I?

When the initial agreement for therapy was made with Jane, I was still living in South Africa practising from an Integrative Humanistic base, although at the time I would have been hard put, even then, to have described what I mean by integrative.

I was educated in South Africa in a Psychology Department that had produced some of the best behaviourists of their generation, at a time when behaviourism was beginning to flourish in university settings with the need to establish psychology as a scientific discipline.

As a student, however, many of us were attracted to psychology because of our interest in people and we found our education in the human sciences to be heavily loaded with experimental psychology and animal behaviour laboratories. I remember, in fact, little from my undergraduate days except being somewhat bored and frustrated by the majority of topics that we studied.

After working for a few years in a research setting, I was offered a part-time teaching position at the university where I had studied. Thus began a lengthy and fruitful academic life, during which time I had acquired a PhD as well as clinical and research psychology qualifications.

I started off teaching subjects like research methods but I remained interested in the human side of psychology. My doctoral research was on young children's imaginative play.

I had taken some time out of my academic career, having had three children by the time I came to do the doctorate, and my thinking then was that, although I hadn't been working seriously for a number of years, I had spent that time being with and observing young children doing what they do. In many ways it seems the natural way of dovetailing the longstanding interest I had acquired into creativity, imagination and imaginative play, with the stage of life that I was at.

Thus I came to teach developmental psychology at both the undergraduate and postgraduate levels. These courses included topics such as Piaget, Bruner and the cognitive theorists of cognitive development as well as Erik Erikson and the more social/emotionally based theorists.

Even at the time, I remember being intrigued by the fact that Piaget's brilliant contribution had ignored the child's social/emotional world. And I felt strongly the need for an approach that would link up and integrate thoughts, feelings and behaviour.

South Africa, at the time when I was studying and in the subsequent years, became more and more violent, politically problematic and turbulent. As academics, we suffered from a brain drain and later academic and intellectual boycotts were affecting us and the quality of our work.

On the other hand, and perhaps as a compensation, we became very well read as a group of professionals and academics, although certain contemporary ideas were not easily available or accessible to us. There were no psychoanalysts in the country and we knew that the most important part of that deprivation was the loss of that kind of thinking. We tried to compensate and make up for this through reading, but we needed the exposure and the possibility of working with psychoanalysts to move our understanding beyond intellectual knowledge to something that could be translated into clinical practice. Further, as can be imagined, much of the psychotherapy then was behaviourally based in the universities and in the mental health institutions.

In line with the so-called 'third wave' being either humanistic or existential psychology, and psychotherapy primarily in the US, there were some practitioners in South Africa who not only experimented with but also taught themselves Transactional Analysis and Gestalt therapy. Then, towards the end of the 1970s and in the early 1980s, a number of us started traveling, largely to the United States, in order to train in these humanistically based, more active, approaches to psychotherapy. During this time there was a smattering of family therapy and also some client-centred therapy work in South Africa.

With a small group of friends and colleagues we formed a TA/ Gestalt society with the main aim of bringing those international trainers who were willing to come out to South Africa, to provide personal/professional training, supervision and an opportunity for some personal work.

Most of us were reasonably well functioning and so we could manage the regressions, crossed boundaries and mixing of personal and therapeutic relationships that occurred as a consequence of that approach to therapy. But it took me a long time to understand that what worked so well for me and for my colleagues was not necessarily going to be good for patients and clients, whose early experience had been seriously damaging, depriving and abusive. Further, the impact of crossed relationships and boundaries was also not clear to me since my experience, which is what therapists base a lot of their understanding on, had been that these could be rationally managed.

As the political situation in South Africa deteriorated, those of us who had done some work with crisis counselling began to understand that we were dealing with something far more serious than crisis intervention. Thus was born the trauma work that was to have a profound influence on my clinical approach and understanding. Through the situation in the country we started to see people soon after traumatic events, and therefore often in a state of emotional high arousal.

The training in regression work, and managing high levels of affect, stood me in good stead for my subsequent work with Jane. People who are immediately post trauma are in states of high arousal and also internally regressed. They need and welcome someone taking charge, and not only telling them what to do but also helping them to manage what feels like unmanageable states of emotion.

By the time I came to England, as I have described above, I had been in practice for a number of years. I had worked long-term with a number of patients (I called them clients) as well as many and various brief interventions. Also, I had done a lot of work in groups, including group therapy, largely of the 'hot seat' variety (individual pieces of work in a group setting where the group forms an audience or chorus), and at the time different group members identify with the person doing the work. With the benefit of my current thinking about the unconscious processes in groups, I feel that individuals in these kinds of processes work on behalf of others as they do the work.

The most influential factors on my clinical practice at that time were those training and intellectual experiences as a backdrop, with the strong influence of the trauma work incorporated into expressive acting out work. I had only an intellectual and sketchy clinical appreciation of the importance of boundaries, containment and transference and counter-transference.

Although I had studied Winnicott's writing for a long time, and taught his ideas of early development to clinical students, I can now say that I had only an intellectual and therefore superficial understanding of the clinical meaning of his complicated concepts.

The idea of the 'use of an object', which is so pertinent to this story of Jane's therapy, is an example of this. It is one of those extraordinary ideas that comes from early development and has direct relevance to clinical work of this nature.

I had been teaching courses to clinical students on the relevance of early development for subsequent adult functioning. It is highly likely that the way I was able to understand and describe early developmental processes, talking about young children and being informed by Winnicott's evocative ideas and poetic language, that gave Jane the sense and hope that I might be able to understand something of her internal chaos when she first heard me teach developmental theories.

Finally I want to say something about the re-decision work as a model for therapy and its usefulness. I was conceptualising the work with early damage, from the perspective of Transactional Analysis, as deficits and trauma lying in the Child Ego State. Other contemporary approaches mention similar notions such as the 'inner child'.

It was assumed that therapy required cathecting those states of mind, or consciousness, then working in the therapeutically induced regression to address and meet some of the unmet childhood needs. That approach, the so-called re-decisional one, works well with people who have well-structured personalities or strong ego defences, being able to hold two realities at the same time. The notion that the child makes a decision about the self and others, in order to cope with the unmet relational need, is one that patients and clients can accept cognitively. Thus the idea that they can re-decide about self and others, once the earlier decision has been surfaced, is readily accepted.

Some of that approach, informed and uninformed both by theory and practice, will become evident in the early stages of the work described below. Also, the progress of the therapy documents my growing and increasing understanding of a different way of looking at, and hence working with, this kind of early disturbance.

There is something that is created in the transference, and beyond the transference, which seems to suggest that the relationship factor is central to a positive outcome in long-term individual therapy. What was of prime importance was that Jane and I established the central elements of this in our therapeutic relationship which included trust, commitment to the work and the process, and a deep level of authenticity.

In concluding this introduction to the story, I finally need to express my deep gratitude to the patient for her tolerance and belief in me and in the process of our work together. And, again, I am also deeply grateful to Patrick Casement whose invaluable support, commitment and unfailing encouragement was central to the development and outcome of the therapy.

Chronology

Having initially told the story of Jane's therapy, the following chapters deal with the various elements that seem to be the central features of the work, as identified both by her and by me as the key aspects of it. I have organised these by examining her letters, written through the major part of the therapy and identifying the repeated themes that emerged.

I will finish this part with a chronology so that the timeline and sequence of events doesn't get lost in the various aspects then to be described. This timeline is to help the reader locate where the material comes from in the chronology of the therapy, thereby hopefully mitigating some of the confusion that becomes inevitable when the chronology is disturbed in the service of describing the use and meaning of the various components of the work. In the text that follows I will from time to time refer to these phases.

First Phase

Initial meeting, the early stages of the work. Primarily a re-parenting phase with strong presentation of the 'little girl/better mother' sequences.

Second Phase

Through the second and third years. Still primarily in the re-parenting mode from which dealing with breaks, gaps and other clients, students and supervisees known to her becomes increasingly difficult.

Third Phase

Two powerful and important influences impacting and changing the course of the therapy towards the end of the third year and throughout the fourth year. These are the introduction of the art therapy and the change in supervision to working with Patrick Casement as supervisor.

Fourth Phase

Having felt that the re-parenting approach was not producing any further productive changes, I understood that I needed to be thinking in another way. The work was then defined by my re-finding the boundaries in order to enable Jane to use me differently.

I refer here to Winnicott's idea that she needed to be able to use me as a representation of the 'failing mother' rather than to struggle to keep me as an idealised mother. What this meant clinically was that she was able to express a lot of aggression and violence towards me as I came to represent, in her mind, the mother who neglected and failed her. In so doing she became more integrated, much of the earlier dissociation disappeared, and she became more and more functional. During this phase Jane left a dysfunctional marriage and then embarked on establishing a sustainable, enriching and satisfying marriage.

Final Phase

Ending, finishing, working through to a good outcome. Tying up the loose ends.

Structure of the book

The next three chapters focus on the primary transference relationship which I described as the 'little girl/better mother' (Chapter 2). In the early part of the therapy this was the idealised transference resting strongly on Jane's wish for a better mother. This is followed by a chapter (Chapter 3) on the impact of the art therapy which significantly opened up the change in the transference as it became no longer possible to split the good from the bad into two therapists. I then follow this with the changed transference (Chapter 4). The chapter on supervision (Chapter 5) mentions aspects of the work from various points, once I began supervision with Patrick Casement.

Finally, Chapter 6 is specifically devoted to the letters and comes with extracts from various places where Jane specifically mentions her experience of writing to me during the therapy.

These later chapters (5 and 6) on supervision and the use of letters – come after the three that deal with the progression of the work. I have risked here losing some of the chronology as this by now has been well established in the earlier sequences.

Logically I finish with a chapter on the ending of the work (Chapter 7) and finally one highlighting a few of the major theoretical ideas that have underpinned the therapy (Chapter 8).

Notes

1 This experience could have happened to Jane as a child in that her mother could have gone (depression, illness, another baby) and come back as a different mother to the young child.
2 In other words my creating the conditions for her to *find me* as the better mother rather than my continuing to be the failing 'better mother'.

Chapter 2

Little girl and better mother

The early phase: re-parenting model

I have called this chapter 'Little girl and better mother' because that wording captures something about the quality of the work from its inception. The therapy was based on the premise, both in the patient's mind and mine, that the route to cure was the reparative experience.

The description of the work in this chapter lays the basis for describing the shifting transference relationship between us as a major shift in understanding and conceptualisation of the therapy that was to occur. It rests on Jane's experiences, both in writing and in the sessions, of being regressed and feeling like a young child in relation to me.

Through this chapter and Chapter 4, I trace how the transference became transformed as I changed in style, largely through the change in supervision and consequentially through my changed view about what this therapy needed in order to bring it to a successful conclusion. I will extract some of these sequences from the letters to illustrate how Jane was experiencing the therapy. Up to a certain point in the work this was primarily how the therapy could be described and how it was proceeding. I have used the term 'better mother' therapy to describe that common approach, which was well developed by Transactional Analysts at the time. The widely held view was, and in fact still is, that the main problem can be thought of as inadequate parenting, and that it can be solved by some form of re-parenting.

Although seemingly simplistic and somewhat grandiose it remains a very compelling and appealing phantasy, often fitting the client/ patient's deepest wish, established in childhood, to find another and a better mother. It is a very comfortable role for a therapist. Many share that wish for themselves, and by projecting the unmet early needs onto a patient they may fulfil their own desire vicariously. It also keeps the therapist in the comfortable and superior position of believing that they can/would have done a better job of looking after the child's needs. The result is that it often keeps the patient stuck in the compliant, 'sweet' child role.

The power of that phantasy is well illustrated by a common slogan carried on T-shirts in California in the 1970s, saying: 'It's never too late to have a happy childhood'. Sadly it is. If you didn't have a good experience as a child you can't really recover those years and have the idealised childhood you missed. The task of therapy is, instead, to help you recover from the past failures and traumas in childhood, to understand the consequences for your adult life, and to ensure that you don't carry it forward on to another generation – but to help you make the most of your adult life from now on.

This section follows the sequence of the letters, from the re-parenting style of therapy to the impact and her distress and resistance as I began to change direction. By shifting gear and becoming more available to be used as a representation of the cold, withdrawing failing mother, I provided Jane with the possibility of using me to represent that mother connecting her to the experience of feeling rejected and unacceptable to that mother. That negative transference began to escalate, following this change in the work, to the point where it was very difficult for both of us to trust that the therapy would not break down. Jane also felt, however, that the long period of good experience had allowed her to develop some trust in my care for her, my good intention and my competence as a therapist. I will discuss this further in Chapter 5.

However, I did not start the work with that perspective. In the early part of the work I was doing my best to provide the 'better' experience. I therefore begin here by focusing on some of those sequences, through Jane's eyes and her letters.

Starting in the 'good mother' phase a poignant description of the little girl followed from a long letter in which Jane described her state of mind. (I wondered to myself whether there is such a thing as a frozen ego state, a state of mind that is developmentally stuck.)

When Jane regressed, she came to feel herself to be that frozen persona. Jane herself is very sure that the re-parenting which she felt herself to be getting at that stage in the therapy was what she needed and made up for the deficits she experienced. The picture she gives us of her childhood shows how children can come to the conclusion that there is something wrong with them and they then find what they see as 'evidence' for their badness.

In a letter from the early phase of the work she says of herself:

> I did hate that frozen, odd secretive, lying stupid socially inept little girl. I had a glimpse of what it could have been for her – maybe she really can have an experience with you that makes a difference to her. She loves you so much, hangs on your every word. She loved being with you whilst you drew in her book ... but is scared you will get angry with her that she is too scared to draw ... It is as though she is there in the shadow but not 'fully' in me ... I can tell I look normal, no-one can see.

The letter also illustrates how she reports on the regressed state, imagining herself to be the little girl although she is not totally regressed. The letter is written with an adult hand, so to speak. However in a session at this point in the work she asks: 'Why can't the little girl talk to you directly?'

There had been a lot of communication to me via letters, a comfortable and comforting state of relating. Although often wordless in the sessions, the letters from this period described in language her experience.

> I have been wondering why the little girl cannot talk to you directly – and what I realise is that she can't speak – she is mute. Mostly she just influences how I feel – it is rarely that she takes over my body, like today. She is usually around to get hurt.
>
> I am going to stop worrying about what is real and isn't real and just tell you my truth ... I was really touched by your care today – you felt like my mummy. I really feel connected to you these days ... There is no way I can do it without a sense of being safely connected to you 'belonging' to you, being your 'little girl' – as well as a grown woman.

Although it was clear to me in the sessions that she was regressed, at times, speaking softly and childishly, it is in these letters that her inner state is so graphically portrayed. The post-session letters from these periods in the work most commonly elaborate the 'little girl' sequences. They were usually written in a coffee shop, after the two-hour session and her long trip to London, where she would go for breakfast to process and recover from the impact of the session.

> ½ little ½ grown drinking hot chocolate and waiting for eggs on toast. The little girl is delighted – she feels as though she has actually been on a picnic with you and to the pool. She also feels a bit bad because she didn't tell you the whole truth about that dress incident....

This extract is a good illustration of how I had assumed the 'role' of the 'good mummy', providing good experiences (in imagination) for the 'little girl'. In fact I felt rather stuck, a bit awkward and scratching around in some way to make contact and relate to a very regressed, often almost wordless and yet quite obviously highly upset, distressed and frightened patient. The 'little girl' sequences provided an emotionally gratifying and ready connection and she seemed unable to get enough of this experience, as well as confirming in letters like this their value to her.

> She knew inside she was a horrible bad person – she only looked 'good' on the outside. After that the little girl told lots of lies. She still gets scared you will get impatient. Like everyone especially her mummy – she was frightened ... She is frightened now that you will not like her any more ... I tell her that you understand – if she told you a lie when she was a little girl, that you probably would have been cross – but you wouldn't have hated her for ever....
>
> The little girl wants more – even if she can only watch from afar. I really know that it is her that desperately needs help – she is very sick – but you must be enormously patient because it may be a long time before she can make a direct appearance again ... she is not sorry that you address her directly – you need to keep doing it she may be in hiding – keeping safe. What frightens her is you may give up. She wants you to know she likes you and she likes the fact that you are interested in her, she wants you to keep talking to her ... She is mute with everyone else. She only talks to me. She is with me right now – I can feel her half in my body and half out ... I have tried all these years to cure her but she is no better. I have never had the

> safety within which to work with her. I do believe at last this is the place, you are the person who will allow the little girl the time and space she needs ... she can't wait to see the nice lady again – wants to see her drawing book ... wonders what the nice lady will draw this time.

This letter is describing some of the quality of playing and 'role playing' from the session. These experiences included drawing, reading from books written for young children and some story telling of imaginatively described experiences like going for a picnic. I also think it is important to recognise that the reparative sequences allowed for childhood memories to surface, and particularly for the expression of the unmet childhood needs.

The problem with the 'better mother' therapy is that meeting the needs in the present is not enough to heal the early damage to the self. What remains unhealed in that work is access to, and the possibility of understanding, the negative emotional consequences for the child as a reaction to their experience of repeated rejection and neglect.

> I realise that you are doing exactly what the 'little girl' needs – to be allowed to be near you – to have you talk gently to her – not to expect her to do anything. She loves the fact that you are prepared to go at her pace ... She wishes you were her mummy – she might get into trouble if her mummy knew she loved you so much ... She doesn't want to use the crayons but likes it when you do. She is always sad even when she is happy she is sad ... She'd like her brother to come too ... He makes it worth staying alive ... Her early memories are of him....
>
> For me I feel less anxious about what is real ... maybe I can relax and let you deal with reality....

Jane is finding a voice for the 'frozen child' who had no way of expressing her needs and suppressed herself. In this way the early childhood memories of trauma began to surface. What began to emerge is a picture of an emotionally deprived and neglected child

> I am pulled between two worlds – the world of the little girl – and the very painful experience she is having with you ... leaving you is hard for her ... she knows that you know how to treat

> little girls and she can just be with you ... I think the little girl that you meet has not yet become repulsive. Somehow when she is with you, she seems like a normal little girl, except that she can't play and gets sad when you are kind to her. Kindness is painful.
>
> There are those with whom the 'odd' uncomfortable little girl is never triggered and those with whom she is a shadowy presence waiting to take over.

At this moment she is describing two forms of the 'little girl', the one presenting to me and the other which some acquaintances and colleagues, at times, experience and respond to. (One that I haven't yet seen but that some people in her circle find irritating and respond to by being quite aggressive to her, or rude.)

> What is important to the little girl, is doing ordinary things with you – the things that make up a day, things which are the background, the fabric of her experience....

What comes to mind here is Pine's (1985) notion of 'moments' and 'background' in development. She is in touch with and describing the quality of her childhood, the atmosphere and climate of harshness, neglect, no sensitivity for a sensitive child, the lack of warmth, gentleness, concern, consideration and patience for the child.

The state of mind that she was in is a 'regressed one'. I had not been active in 'making' her regress. At this time in the work, both she and I were working from a TA model which assumed that the 'inner child', the Child Ego State, or states, can be activated or accessed throughout our adult lives. It was also her experiential reality. We shared a language to describe the experience. It had psychological and phenomenological validity as well as giving credence to the notion that early states become frozen and can be recaptured in their entirety.

Here is a post session extract from the first phase, by which time Jane's habit of writing frequently and after sessions was well established:

> I am still regressed, frightened, overwhelmed, it is all too difficult ... The little girl needs to grow up in her life to deal with the world ... I need you so much it frightens me ... will I

recover from this? Will she recover something of who she might have been?

Later in the same letter she adds:

> You probably feel that I am asking too much and I am clear that I am not asking to be included in your actual family but that you will hold me in your heart, as an adopted daughter rescued from a bleak and terrible orphanage and given a loving home.

Jane shows again her capacity for using language and metaphor to capture the emotional need and the wished-for relationship. This is a powerful illustration of the consequences of the 'better mother' therapy. The evocation of what feels like a 'primary attachment' and the dependency fostered.

If the work had finished at this point it would have been another incomplete therapy. Jane felt and believed that enough of this ongoing creation of the good experience would eventually help the 'inner child' and repair the early damage.

I was by now exceedingly concerned by her level of dependency, and how to resolve or 'grow' the internal little girl without the years of going through the normal developmental processes that real children require.

The missing understanding that I didn't have at this point in the therapy, which was to prove to be crucial to the ultimately successful outcome, was how to deal with the inevitable failure of the re-parenting and the consequences of the disillusionment and the patient's disappointment. The essence of this manuscript is to show how I acquired the understanding that could change the therapy, achieving what we both wished for but were trying to do from a mistaken premise.

Before returning to the main transference relationship, and how this changed from the 'little girl' seeking a 'better mother', I will describe the impact that the art therapy had on the work. We had decided together to introduce an experience of art therapy with an experienced art therapist, as a holding therapy during my long break in the winter of the third year of our therapy. The next chapter deals with that specifically as it was to prove to be a significant element in the overall work, and contributed in a powerful way to the resulting changes that occurred in the transference relationship.

Chapter 3

The impact of the art therapy

The art therapy was introduced slightly before the long break towards the end of the third year of therapy. The introduction of the art therapy was going to prove to be very powerful to the work, and aided the course of the therapy dramatically. Initially it was introduced as a way of providing Jane with some therapeutic support during the winter while I was going to be away.

In discussing the gap at the end of the third year of the therapy, Jane suggested doing some art therapy, as a 'holding' possibility. It was her idea. Rather naïvely, I think, we both initially thought of it as something different, creative and in some ways lighter – a form of 'play' therapy, in preference to the long, dark trips to London in the middle of winter to see another talking therapist, who would keep focusing her on her distress and sense of abandonment.

It seemed to both of us that Jane could engage in a possibly colourful and enjoyable activity. Neither of us could predict what was going to be opened up and unleashed in that work; further, she suggested starting the art therapy some time before I left, seeing both of us for a while.

The early letters which refer to the art therapy were while I was still in London, as Jane decided to begin working with an art therapist before I left. I saw this as her needing support and encouragement from me to begin this new venture.

> I feel a secret bubble of joy – mixed with a large dose of anxiety about the Art Therapist. I have really found a home ... for now I welcome a temporary sanctuary in your heart....

Very quickly Jane began to feel all sorts of unexpected things, became scared of what she was experiencing and was in some ways beginning to feel as if she were 'unravelling':

I was disturbed and frightened – I need you to know what is happening, to see, to know ... maybe see some of the 'mess' I have made and left for her. This week I stayed grown up, moulded clay, not throwing it, painted and used pastels. I talked to her about feeling as though what I did was abusive. She didn't really comment – but stayed warm and close to my experience ... I feel as though you have sent me away to boarding school and I can see that I could learn a lot, but I miss you so much and need you to come and talk to the teacher, see my work ... How will I manage at boarding school for so long – when I am still little and need my mummy?

Your confused and confusing 'daughter'.

Her ending her letter in this way shows how firmly it was written in the 'little girl' mode.

The unstructured, non-verbal nature of the art material, and attractive nature of the setting, provides an invitation to express and to experience something of one's self, always provoking unconscious aspects of one's internal world. In Jane's case, given that this opportunity was so directly linked to our work and to the pain in the work we were engaged in, it should have been more apparent to us that it was going to be both significant and powerful in relation to her therapy. The art therapist was an experienced therapist who was used to providing space, materials and encouragement for self-expression in the work.

Most of the letters to do with the art were written to me in the 'little girl' vein. We had both identified the 'little girl' as around four. Here she directly describes her as that age.

Very early in the process of the art therapy, Jane connected with how art work unleashes, and at the same time puts her in touch with, her primitive phantasies which she had thought of as her 'madness'. Equally the dissociation, which was her defence against fragmentation and a form of disintegrating, can be seen as out of touch with present shared reality.

It was particularly the very young, the primitive and the violent parts that emerged in Jane's relationship with me, dealing with me and the on-going strain of the therapy. The real external stresses in the work were to do with, on the one hand, the breaks and gaps when I was away or not able to see her. Jane was also being exposed to, and needing to deal with, other professional relationships of mine that she knew about, particularly those in her own professional sphere. Unleashing her suppressed feelings allowed for the negative transference, her images and phantasies of me, to emerge and become powerfully present – keeping her in a constant state of conflict.

Jane, being such a psychologically sophisticated observer, quickly understood some of the ways in which art therapy can be used and is helpful to patients. She identifies how she enters with some feeling of choice about what she will do, and yet she also describes how powerful the process is and how she can feel taken over by it. In addition, while she was working with both of us, she felt the support of being held by two therapists. Furthermore, out of awareness initially, she uses the opportunity it provides to split, continuing to attempt to keep me 'good', clean and loving, while feeling freer to 'mess' in the other therapy.

> I have been to Art. I arrived tearful (4 years old). X is being treated badly by his mother's new boyfriend and has turned from a sunny, happy, little boy into an angry, unhappy child. The story 'hit' me in the heart – for him, for all children trapped in desperate situations, for me and for all my siblings. I cried ... felt the pain of the helpless child. So this is what I painted today ... Looking at it as an event in this way stopped me from descending into those areas which feel psychotic ... What I am learning is that Art Therapy can be used in many ways – to descend into 'psychosis', to ground experience, to contain frightening feelings – and I am sure more. I wasn't so busy today – usually I paint or create lots of things ... I still feel good about the process ... I like going – I am longing to see you, to tell you, to share something of what is happening.
>
> I feel my helplessness in the face of you ... I am lost with you ... I get very scared. Am a bit scared that you will be repulsed or disgusted at the mess I make ... I am glad of you, glad of the Art – I can let myself feel safely held with the two of you – and twice a week feels so secure ... I am terrified of the gap.

Once she began working with the art therapist we continually referred to her art work in sessions and spoke about what was going on there. Some of my early notes include this conversation about the art. She repeated to me how pleased she was that I and the art therapist had been in contact and also that I had seen some of her pictures. We agreed that she would bring them to her session with me. It was already clear to me that whatever is happening in the art therapy needed to be integrated into our work, although I was not sure at that time how to enable that.

The other problem, which we discussed a number of times, was who the art therapist represented in her mind, in other words, how to interpret or understand the place the art therapist had taken in our work. She is not the 'other parent'. That role was the one Jane's supervisor took. We speculated that the art therapist could be like a teacher, in her mind, as she spoke about going to school. She then told me about how a teacher had smacked her in the second grade, and she believes this inhibited her, that it had interfered with her ability to concentrate and perform well academically.

I think the constant strain Jane was under, as a frightened and bullied child, contributed to her struggles at school. She was told at school and also by her mother that she wasn't capable of doing anything, and she left school as soon as she could, at sixteen, to take up training as a nurse. This was not a happy time for her. She stayed on to finish, to the point where she could train to get a job and be able to leave home. As we talked about her early school days she connected to how scared she was at school. She then decided that the art therapist was some sort of 'nanny', a child-minder.

In a letter Jane says to me:

> I don't want to deal with my anger towards her. I just want to go and paint my pictures and go away, come to you for connection, 'blank' her out – I have this image of the three of us together. Turning my back on her and focusing on you. As I write this I feel more and more negative towards her – it is painful to go there – I am embarrassed and ashamed by what has happened. She has seen me – seen the mess and chaos. She has seen what no one else has ever witnessed – how can I have a relationship with her after that?

None of this material had surfaced between us yet, and this was the first indication that I had about the extent of the violent and primitive nature of those images. They would necessarily come into our work and the art therapy provided us with the bridge for our talking therapy

> The images come back again. I dump everything on her – get rid of the unspeakable, the poison, the rotting flesh, the terrible nauseating smell – leave it and come to you. This process is bigger than me – at times controlling me. I have always needed you to know. What worries me is the amount of poison I contain. I could pour it out now. Pages and pages of poison.

And then the next day:

> I realise that I have kept the rageful, destructive, angry self away from you ... I am very frightened my rage would destroy your good will towards me ... How can I be in a position of conflict with you ... I know that some of my pictures are full of poison, of rage, of despair and anguish – what else can I do?

So the art therapy had opened up the way to experience, channel and communicate these raw, unprocessed feelings. It had provided us with the raw material to keep making sense of her early relationships and how these haunt her adult life.

> I am aware that I am dealing with my mad self. This is what I need to do in therapy ... bring you my madness, it is in the letters, in the terror that makes up so much of my relationship with you ... as I wrote you appeared before me dressed in black, dripping in blood ... The censor has a hard time operating in the Art therapy and right now my urge to be mad is very strong. Those therapies that emphasised the Adult enabled me to function but left the madness untouched.
> It is my madness I lay before you – my mad self needs healing. I first encountered my 'mad child' on a Re-Childing workshop where she wanted to destroy everything and was dealt with severely, rightly so ... I can barely wait till she can 'splurge' out on paper. I need to 'pour out' in these letters to you. I could work for ever on my 'sane' self, helping me cope in the real world – but the real healing has to be with all these children. The mad ones, the sane ones, the grey baby.
> Mostly now I write to the Diana I see ... But the Art work has tapped areas of myself which need to be in the field between us. So I am glad to bring the pictures to you – I know that this is still indirect but it is the best I can do.

We now had a forum and a means of expression which was going to prove to be one of the turning points of the work, by finding a way of unleashing and expressing the 'madness' and then being able to bring it to me. The madness seemed to be made up of her unprocessed and uncontained rage, going back to her earliest experience, as well as (most likely) that of her mother and grandmother: and, as Jane says, going back over generations of deprivation, abuse and unmet relational as well as material needs.

This work, begun some weeks before I left London for a break, continued until some weeks after my return in the early spring.

I introduce here some notes made after a session (set in italics), towards the end of the year shortly after she started the art therapy, in which she had brought some of her art work to show me.

Jane began by speaking of the train journey, the work she had done the previous week-end, and then about her childhood experience of 'hovering' around her mother, unable to go but also unable to do anything else, her mother's contempt and how she would dissociate from it. She spoke about her supervisor and about the friend she was staying with in London. I commented on the 'atmosphere', the emotional climate she often felt she was subjected to as a child. That the abuse was indirect and intangible ... Also commented on how in the other relationships she had mentioned she carried some of that inadequate sense of self with her ... I continued with 'When there is something more specific it is easier to defend yourself from being attacked, even internally by telling yourself certain things. These indirect attacks were defended by dissociation from the present.'

There was then a pause in the session and Jane turned to the paintings she had brought with her. I made some associations as I looked at these paintings which were abstract, quite colourful. As I did this she began to disconnect from me and seemed to go into a distancing and internal state in the room, saying she doesn't know what is scaring her.

I say I wonder if she is scared about what I will either notice or attend to. So perhaps we should just look at them. And I stopped commenting on the pictures to her. The pictures, as I looked more closely, engendered a feeling of desolation and bleakness, descriptors she uses often of her experience of her childhood. They did indeed echo a comment I had made about the bleakness of her childhood. She then says: 'They are of me. When I go the world is without me in it.' I understood her to be describing a sensation of losing herself and not knowing 'who she is' by this statement.

Jane then talks of connecting with the rage. There is a good deal of red in the centre of several of the pictures. Continuing, she describes how she can't control the process: how the experience stirs up very primitive, violent, frightening and overwhelming phantasies: that she becomes gripped with a wish to destroy, to smash to break and crush....
I said perhaps that is what she wishes to do here.
She replied:

> It was repressed and has always felt to be inexpressible and uncontainable

This is the beginning of how Jane is finding a way to express what has been repressed and has always felt unexpressible and uncontainable.
In a letter she had said:

> When I leave here [her session with me] the world is empty. I feel empty but uncontrollably rageful.

(This became the beginning of my emotional exposure to, rather than a report back of the experience of, absence (abandonment) – the vanishing and uncontaining mother, which was to become such a strong feature of the future work.)
I comment on the value of my seeing the pictures, as they seem to have a lot to do with our process. Jane agrees but remains in this session somewhat agitated. I speculated that this was embarrassment at suddenly feeling that she had exposed more than she wanted to, or was in her control.
(I understood now that one of the challenges would be to get the material from the art therapy into our sessions.)
I continue by saying that by bringing the drawings to our session Jane is making me a part of that work. I further wonder what she imagines my reaction to her work is. She immediately responds that I view it (she assumes) with contempt. I challenge her by asking if that is really how she might be reading my response. At that point she says no and she is pleased that she showed them to me and we have talked about them like this.
In the next session, that closely followed this one, shortly before my departure at the end of the year, Jane started being angry with the art therapist, her supervisor and of course me.

As we talk about my pending departure, Jane speculates that the art therapist is 'the Child Minder'. While she is talking about this she is sucking her fingers in a self-soothing way. She says here in this session that she is able to put things in the letters that she can't say directly to me.

Jane had drawn her supervisor as a 'sheep dog'. I wondered with her then who she may be in her mind. Here too there is some notion of being 'minded' by another in my absence. Fortunately, as it turns out, this transference figure is benign and helpful to her and her development.

For the main extent of the art therapy, during the time when I was away, we had negotiated proper sessional timed phone calls, usually lasting 50 to 55 minutes on a weekly basis. In the phone calls Jane did not appear to be regressed and we had reasonable conversations. The calls were regular, felt containing and provided her with a sense of continuity and connectedness to me that seemed to be holding up well.

Of course, what was happening at that time was that her distress and 'madness' were being poured out on paper and to a large extent kept away from me. However, at one point I received a worried phone call from the art therapist. Although I did not fully understand what the therapist's concern was about, clearly the psychotic and extremely violent material that was to emerge in the letters was now in Jane's art work. It became more and more evident to me that my clinical challenge was going to be to enable that material to be expressed to me, firstly by way of letters and then eventually directly in the sessions, face-to-face.

In a letter, written to me during the break and before my return, Jane says:

> I suddenly feel a flash of anger towards you. You are so far away ... It is hard to maintain this long distant connection. I didn't manage to plug into this morning and the recharging didn't work.

When I reflected on the sessional notes shortly after my return I realised, now that I had returned, that Jane probably felt we had a long time together before the next break. She began to feel safer and more able to put things directly to me in our sessions.

Sessional notes early in the fourth year

Jane comes in and says, unusually: 'Hello Diana' making direct and immediate contact ... She talks about her friends and colleagues that may know me, but especially her friend who was working with me at the time in some of the training groups I was running. This leads to memories of mother and sister. I say that being the preferred child didn't necessarily serve her sister any better than being the non-preferred child, as evidenced by her sister's disturbance and difficulties. Jane continues, however, with how she longs for attention and to feel 'special' ... finally, after a bit more of a preamble, she gets to the point where she becomes emotional and talks about the difficulty of waiting for me, and reconnecting with me now that I am home.

Soon after this fairly calm session, Jane writes one of the most psychotic and violent letters. I noted that this letter was really an example of 'the violence unleashed' and that the content in the art material was coming closer to where it needed to be located, with me. Helpfully too, this was now translated into language, allowing for the meaning to be better understood consciously by both of us.

> Need to write, need to paint, need to immerse, to be wild, uncontrolled ... Don't forget the wild thing. Disturbed, deranged, crazy, mad ... My body courses with electricity of derangement – energising, burning ... Seeing you touched that place, wanting to hurt, harm, cut bite ... A visitor from another place ... looking and sounding human. My friends are profane, depraved ... Need you to know, to hold, to see, to hear, to smell ... don't turn away

I then made the following notes, for issues to be raised in supervision about the treatment and problems in therapy:

1 *The here-and-now situation. The problem of the boundaries and holding them in a number of ways.*
2 *How to get the material that was being evoked, unleashed and expressed in the art therapy, into our work and between us. What to pick up in the sessions and how to work with these issues. With regard to this question I noted that I felt relief at being able to externalise the questions.*
3 *How did the material arise and what does it mean? Was there systematic abuse? Jane's image of self is of one who is poisoned and is poisonous. Who does she feel so bad in relation to? What*

she is now engaged with is self-perpetuating and confirming how she poisons herself.
4 *The question of cleanliness. She is interested in dirt. In the material, is the dirt and filth breaking through something that has been repressed? Somehow it is a concretisation of experience, an attempt to capture what was done to her and also an attempt to split off certain experiences.*

Supervision notes and some of my reflections

There are two views of me. On the one hand Jane assumes that I am afraid of the material, as afraid of her craziness as she is. What becomes important here is the experience of being with someone who can understand this anxiety. She keeps it out of the session by writing about it.

On the other hand she is inviting me to treat it as if it were not real. That I can easily slip into the role of supporting her at the expense of not staying with the difficulties.

Jane is showing me that she contains within her very disturbing elements, and what she needs from me is to deal with these without deflecting from them or being afraid of them. The question of where they come from is crucial to understanding them. This is an important question which I will need to help her with.

> I write them as I feel the pain ... they [her split off other parts which she calls here the 'little people'] are really scared that you will stop seeing them. As I write this it is a God-given opportunity to put something right, to heal the pain, stake a claim for life, for happiness for my future ... I do at last believe that you would recognise me on the street, remember that I exist ... it doesn't mean the little people don't need evidence that you still know them ... the safety the opportunity to connect with the craziness has no words. I am feeling a mixture of things – clearer, somehow stronger – but scared that the little or crazy parts are assumed to have disappeared....
>
> The art therapy tricked the 'censor' and the mad child escaped, slipped by ... it is less easy now, he [one of the most aggressive ego states, possibly the one she described as 'the devil child'] knows he can keep the madness locked up by choosing certain material and avoiding others ... However he will destroy all the small activity by the mad child ... she needs to

be known, to be seen as well as the 'sweet child' ... Writing this letter is such a relief it helps me to think.

Although I will not go mad in the world ... I do need to go mad in therapy, to have my madness seen, known recognised and worked with.

In finding herself able to use art therapy and art materials to express her internal world, Jane has now been able to give form and shape to the 'madness', that which has been completely out of her conscious awareness or has been formless and shapeless till now, but the words in the letters are not quite able to reach the full expression of this either.

And so she came to it herself:

I would like the art room and materials – but you – because this is our therapy ... it's so hard to connect to words. They are clean, precise, organised unmessy. I need to do something physical and I need you. The rush is coming and I've said it all

(but she repeats this anyway).

At about this time she has a dream about someone called 'K', who tells her she is going away for six months but she is 'grown up' enough now. She connects the dream to the art therapist whose name begins with 'K' and says of the art therapist:

She doesn't understand about the babies or 'my need for you'.

I reply that although it is still 6 months till I go away again she is both still dealing with the past and anticipating the future.

I make a note from supervision that there are too many babies for the mother, who experienced them as too much for her. My patient's anxiety and belief is that this would prove too much for me.

Soon after this Jane begins to put into words, and write to me something of, the emotional quality that she had been expressing in the art work. As it was still early spring in that fourth year I was now going to be around for a long period, providing a sense of safety and the space to work in.

As the work continued, and the difficult and loaded material was being more and more explicitly expressed in the letters, in words and to me, the problematic nature of the two therapies was beginning to be resolved.

Sometime after my return in the next spring, Jane decided to give up the art work. It had fulfilled its purpose by bringing into consciousness the horrors, 'the monsters in the mind'. As I had also stopped being the 'better mother' in her mind she could increasingly 'use' me to represent the failing, depriving and persecutory mother. Although this was not immediately spoken about she gave up the art therapy, recognising that there was no further need for her to work with both of us.

The art therapy seemed to have served its purpose, although there had been a thought that Jane might continue with both of us for a while. It became clear that she no longer needed to split us. The process of 'healing the split', or bringing the split parts of the therapists together, had begun. As these became integrated so too was she beginning to heal her own dissociated selves.

Jane was by now able to write rather than draw or paint: 'In touch with blood and gore, the dismembered bits...'.

In Chapter 4 I continue with an account of how the therapy progressed once the art therapy finished.

The break in the work proved to be the last time a 'holding' therapy was needed during my absences abroad. Again, at the time it wasn't immediately obvious but once the material that had been expressed in the art could come directly to me, first in letters and then also directly in the sessions, Jane became able to give up the art therapy quite easily. The art therapist herself recognised that it had served its purpose, as a 'holding' process and as a bridge to what needed to surface from Jane's mind, to be directed at the person I had become in her mind.

In summary then, the art therapy allowed Jane to find a way to express the bad and angry destructive feelings directly to me, and in so doing start a process of bringing good and bad together in her mind. Healing the splits between good and bad, acceptable and unexpressible, she was also able to give up dissociation as a major defence and let go some of the split off states – becoming increasingly integrated.

The art therapy worked together with the supervision which supported me both in understanding what was happening, and therefore containing the direct attacks, thus creating the optimal conditions for Jane to use me as a representation of the 'failing parent'. I will take this up below in Chapter 5 on the contribution of the supervisor to the therapy, after returning to the clinical sequence, by looking at how the main transference changed.

Chapter 4

The changing transference from idealisation to the failing mother

This chapter deals with the changing transference and escalating anger towards me as it became untenable to split the good and bad between two therapists or keep the 'bad' out of our work. The combination of the introduction of the art therapy in the third break, and the way in which the change in supervision influenced my change in relation to her in the room, taken together, supported the dramatic changes in the transference and Jane's view of me. I deal directly with the way supervision impacted and changed the work in the following chapter although I will refer to it in passing here.

Prior to the introduction of the art therapy, some negative or cross little girl statements began to appear in the letters. Here is a letter written the day after a session (in Phase 2) from the third year, in which Jane continues to share aspects of the 'little girl's' experience, written prior to the art work and the influence of the new supervision with Patrick Casement, who highlighted how I had adopted the good mother stance. In this letter, she is telling me about a structure, built in a forest near where she lives, for children and members of the public to enjoy.

> I am sitting in the fairy house ... The little girl is delighted and she wants you to see. I know you won't agree, but maybe one day you will agree, to come and see the fairy tree ... The little girl is cross again – wants you here now by this tree.
> I don't want to experience this level of need of you for ever ... I think the little girl has settled a bit. I am feeling more 'held'.

As we have seen in the previous chapter, introducing art therapy created the possibility to change, dramatically, the course of the work and to open up the way to move on from the 'idealised mother re-parenting' style of the work by engaging directly with the negative aspects of the transference. Initially a split was created by working with two therapists. The patient could keep her therapist good and make the art therapist the failing therapist. However, by now I was helped and supported by the understanding gained in supervision. Thus I recognised how important it was not only to heal the split but to bring the material from the art work into our sessions.

Then some months later, Jane commented in one of our sessions – still clearly in the little girl mode but after she had begun the art therapy and was seeing both of her therapists (still Phase 2):

> I don't like the sessions where the grown-ups do most of the talking, though I recognise the fact that the grown-ups had things to talk about. I don't want you to relegate the 'little girl' to second place – because she holds the key to healing. It is through her, change is happening.

This extract shows how firmly she was convinced at this stage that the healing would come from being re-parented, from being allowed to redo or grow up almost with another and 'better' mother. In a sense she begins to play with reality again here, and tries to push away the adult reality.

At this time also the letters were complex as there are times when Jane reports on the little girl and times when she writes from that state of mind. The little girl however is no longer only a sweet good child. Some of the other split off parts had become manifest between us. The expression of these dissociated parts remained nonetheless reasonably controlled and verbal, using language with childlike words like 'naughty' to express her distress and anger.

The 'little girl' remained the predominantly reported-on state, but the picture was becoming more complicated and complex, as these various comments show.

> I noticed yesterday that the little girl disappeared when she met your eyes.
>
> I worry when you say that you have made mistakes with me. Was making contact with the grey baby, the pink baby and the little girl a mistake? To me it was an utter relief – at last someone had seen, someone knew.

> I'm stamping and shouting – being very naughty and feel the sting of your slap as you get cross – I even welcome the slap, it is a powerful connection … Time has gone and she is furious – red-faced, kicking screaming, beating you with her fists, biting you, wanting you to take control because she is so scared how out of control she is.

And finally:

> The strange thing is happening recently, no matter what 'part' of me gets your attention, the others feel disappointed. The little girl hates it when she takes a back seat … Good night horrid mummy.

This last extract raised for me the question of 'who drives her?' When is the 'little girl' in charge? She seemed at this time, to be the most powerful of the 'altered states'. Perhaps she was the most conscious and accessible, and the one she 'lived' in most of the time. Here she is warning me of the strain of the therapy, the constant yearning and the ongoing experiences of being abandoned.

As the third year began to draw to an end my therapeutic approach was changing, reflected by how I was in the room with her, primarily under the influence of Patrick Casement. As he increasingly questioned the over solicitousness of the 'good mother', the angry child began to appear more and more strongly.

> The little girl says she is never coming back. She sends you a drawing of how cross she is.

At around this time then Jane's rage, and probably her terror, was becoming conscious and she was able to express these emotions directly to me and about me. She was experiencing me, initially in the absences, and in between sessions ever increasingly, as the 'attacking and failing' mother. Thus the switches themselves are occurring rapidly and are now emerging from the art work into our process.

Jane's anger with me turned into being graphic and destructive, but also primitive rage as shown in this letter somewhat later than the 'horrid mummy' phase.

> The phantasy moves onto a mess of battered and bruised, bleeding bodies. She wants to hurt you today but fears it. Fears that you will move away. A switch now.

As these letters escalated, with increasingly violent images, another thought that I had was that some of these ghastly phantasies were probably in the mother's mind. Thus in addition to her rough handling, sneering at the child and bullying and terrifying her, below the surface, in the mother's mind perhaps there were images of violence and the brutality in her own family.

The mother's family were known to be 'cruel to their animals', so some of the blood and gore could well have been what the mother as a child had witnessed. There could also have been in that family sadistic pleasure at hurting animals and children. Further it was likely that the abuse went back some generations when it would have been easier to escape outside attention and intervention of gross physical abuse of children or animals.

This thinking about the meaning of the images had to do with my trying to make sense of them so that Jane too could begin to understand where these violent thoughts might have come from. My hypothesis was that the images themselves might go beyond her own history to that in previous generations. Such an explanation helps to see some of her mother's behaviour towards her as not necessarily to do with Jane's faults but the mother's own experience of trauma in her childhood.

The second letter that day contains more 'little girl' material, now written more as the 'little girl' directly, as the transference as well as our real interactions have changed in the room. In the change Jane was experiencing me as treating her very badly (see letter below).

> I hate you, I hate you, I hate you ... I'll bite you when I see you, push you over – die – then you'll wish you had read to me. IT'S NOT FAIR! WHY CAN'T I HAVE STORIES AND PICNICS ... WHY?
>
> I don't want you to be my Diana any more – I'll find a new Diana who will not be horrid to me. I'll keep being brought to your house but I won't speak to you ever again! You used to be my friend but you stopped. I want to hurt you.

Although Jane never self-harmed actively by hurting herself physically, she expressed a good deal of pain and distress in letters like this. Through the expression of her anger directly in this way, no longer protecting the therapist, herself and the therapy, she was creating the pathway to integration and health. The fear of retaliation however was still great but gradually, as the material entered into the sessions, her levels of anxiety and agitation decreased.

And then a third letter in as many hours, she says:

> I've lost you Diana, the loss is terrible ... I can't help it if the little girl loves you as her mummy – no matter how you treat her or what you say to her about not being her mummy. The fact is that in her heart you are her mummy.

The difference that now lay between her experience in her early life and our work was being found in that I listened and accepted these feelings, all of them, as unpleasant and nasty as they were in relation to me. Nonetheless they were contained in the letters, and contained by her therapist in that I was not unduly anxious or worried by active self-harming ways of dealing with her agitation and anxiety – now that she could express her rage more directly to me.

In a different letter from this second phase, written immediately after a session, the 'little girl' talks about the dissociation process:

> Feeling a mixture of things – the acute pain of the little girl – mitigated by her observation that you love her ... amid the pain ... feel relief at being seen recognised ... I only know that when you reflect back 'separate selves' the internal experience is one of rightness, of being seen ... I can say that there is no other agenda for me except to be known ... Even though you have changed your approach to the little girl – she loves you so much – she feels joy at the connection ... the pain of the little girl who wants to crawl on your lap and is continually peeled off ... the little girl is cut and bleeding.

And then:

> Awake and in pain haunted by the images of the Robertson film of the little boy (called John) who is sent to a nursery ... I feel that the little girl had started to come alive, to heal, to love and be loved ... Now you are deliberately withholding from her in a way that is terribly cruel ... I don't know if I can keep bringing her again to be shunned, ignored, frozen out ... You allowed the little girl to love you, allowed her to heal – she was healing – and now somehow you think that is wrong ... so you

> stand and watch her disintegrating – dispassionately watch her agony. See her squirm ... She knows it would only take the smallest shift in your hand for you to reach out and she would be comforted.

By now I had moved away from her across the room and had predominantly become the 'withholding cold mother' in her mind. Furthermore as I became increasingly aware of the problems of the 'better mother' approach, I became consciously more neutral in attitude and probably was perceived by her as somewhat cool. Certainly I was careful about being too warm or welcoming, in greeting her. I think the sharp contrast to her previous experience of me now created this sense of rejection and also some confusion.

> The question for me is – how do I know that bringing her each week to be tortured in this way is the right thing? ... I know that this is not persecution in your belief. I trust your integrity and commitment and believe that you think the pain is necessary. That somehow through the agony she will heal. Myself I can't see it. She comes each week with a surge of hope – only to meet your impassivity, withholding and coldness to her.

It was not that I believed the pain was necessary at all. Rather I was now pursuing an approach on the premise that 'more mothering', and playing into the belief that the re-parenting was the route to cure, was not proving effective – blocking any experience of negative transference to emerge between us, and preventing the next stage of development and separation/individuation to occur.

After a number of months well into Phase 3, and as we shifted into Phase 4, the therapy continued to represent the developmental work which was required for her to complete the process of separation and individuation between us. She needed to find her emotional reality, that we indeed have separate and independent minds. This phase was heralded by us becoming engaged in a massive conflict on a number of levels. She argued theoretically and rationally with me about the therapy and also continued to plead from the wounded child.

Thus in the next letter:

> Am not sure the little girl will come and see you any more ... She cannot keep on letting her heart open – all hope is gone ... no more point in saying anything, nothing changes.

And then another letter:

> Because I am talking to you in my head – I thought it would release me from rumination if I write. I am remembering with gratitude what we have done together and the difference in my relationships with others. If we go no further I will always have this. Now I feel sad – that we have opened a door together but cannot do more than that. I still don't believe that I will find anyone else willing to walk that road with me. What I am clear is that re-traumatising the little girl is not OK ... she builds no new experience of feeling worthy of caring and expecting care in return, of joy. She becomes bruised and depressed and touches agony and despair ... The re-traumatising her does bring the work into the room, into the relationship between you and her – but not in any way that is healing... She is too young to make any sense of the change in you – she doesn't understand why she is persecuted and rejected. I feel desperate – this is a mistake and I don't know how to make you listen.

The communication about the pained little girl is still primarily by letter. These words carry a strong flavour of the transferential replay between us, as they could powerfully reflect a young child pleading with her mother who has perhaps become overwhelmed with a new sick and difficult baby, thereby neglecting a sensitive toddler.

In order to give a flavour of how these sentiments presented in a session I include here some extracts from a session about a week or so after these last letters. Jane returned to therapy towards the end of August (in the fourth year) a few weeks after a hysterectomy. This session was also well into the work, the art therapy was finished, and by now I was feeling strongly supported by supervision and much clearer about the direction of the work.

Sessional notes

Jane is in a post-operative state and thus rather fragile and vulnerable. She starts off by saying how confused she feels. She now goes on to talk about the little girl to me. 'I can't keep bringing her here,' she says, despairingly. 'I have a terrible sense of loss about this. And I have to have a conversation with you about it.'

I ask her: 'I wonder if you feel that this change in style is mad making?'

Continuing, Jane stresses: 'You are wrong, wrong!' She can't see how it is either helpful or healing for her to feel the way she is now, towards me or the therapy. Also she has heard me saying I will never hold the little girl again.

I say that my saying 'No' means she isn't getting what she 'wants' that is so painful. However, for me the issue has to do with boundaries and we are arguing about control and who is in control of the work.

Jane carries on, saying that in her experience the 'little girl' no longer comes skipping into sessions. In fact she can't bring her any more. She, the 'little girl', experiences being blanked and dismissed by me, which is as cruel as her mother was to her. She tells me that she tore up a photo she had of me. Also she feels she has grown a lot from wanting to curl up and suck her fingers.

I comment that I had certainly changed my style since my last return in the spring. I was feeling the urgency to work with 'abandonment' and the insecure attachment before the next approaching break in the work. Although only in some months' time I was beginning to be aware of the coming winter break, as I knew she was without us necessarily talking about it yet.

She persisted with this theme, telling me, as in the letters that she doesn't know how she can move forward without bringing the little girl to me.

Such a clear indication of how embedded her image of re-parenting, and the 'better mother', is in her mind and that the therapy comes about through this corrective emotional experience.

She links the mad stuff to the frustration engendered by the deprivation she now feels from me.

I respond that the frustration is precisely what is provoking the anger and that it needs necessarily to be brought to me.

My reflections on this session

By now I had clearly understood how important it is for Jane to be able to use me as a representation of the 'cold withholding, uncaring and not understanding mother'. That she needs to direct at me all these feelings, some real about me, others from the past, with the fullness that she experiences them.

I had become confident and clear now about what was happening, and that it was my task to accept the feelings: neither to deny, retaliate or defend, or to disappear in the face of them. I am working with the thought that, prior to our work together, she hadn't developmentally achieved this stage and now she is beginning to find someone who takes seriously, listens and accepts responsibility for Jane's perceived behaviour towards her.

I am holding my position while at the same time hearing and working towards understanding the impact on Jane and the enormous pain and distress that this causes her. Although I am reading her responses as transferential, at the same time they are also in relation to my real shift in behaviour towards her which can be experienced as withholding and rejecting.

In the next session following the one above:

Jane comes in saying she feels better. She has more perspective and feels she has a choice about going or staying. However she wants help in order to understand what would be in her best interests.

It seems I don't want the little girl any more, that I am telling her to grow up. And she doesn't feel ready to do that yet. On the contrary she feels battered and bruised and unsure.

As the session progresses she speaks about feeling that she can taste blood. How comfortable she feels by these sensations. Comfortable and soothed. How easy it is to get into them. When she connects with the violence and viciousness she becomes terrified of the torturer (within). And then she says the little girl is scared of me now and my capacity to abuse her.

Reflecting on how her mood was constantly shifting:

I thought that, at this point in the therapy, Jane was clearly believing that she needs to split in order to protect herself. She is still using the defence of dissociation. The supervision, which consistently supported me with the idea that I needed to be around for these feelings, was of course also strengthening the idea that the negative feelings could be heard, tolerated and contained, and didn't need to be excluded in order to remain acceptable and in the relationship.

I can't afford to feel it as a little girl.

And she continues to write:

> The little girl can't even bear to think of you. I have forever avoided the pain she needs to face, in the pain she is truly alone.
> If I thought it would help – I am committed 100% and – I don't want any more of this – I want out, want to go to someone else, anyone – it's too tough – I don't know what would have happened if you had continued to love the little girl. Would she have blossomed and flowered? Or would she allow it. But I really believe you are wrong. That re-traumatising her does bring the work into the room, into the relationship between you and her – but not in any way that is healing ... She is too young to make sense of the change in you ... The difficulty is, without her I don't know what we can do. She is an integral part of the process.

And then some months later in a post session letter:

> I am in the 'Coffee Cup' feeling my body to be bruised and battered. I also feel very ashamed and somewhat 'restored' by the contact.

Before finishing this year and going through another winter break I had these reflections. The letters had become very disturbing and I was certainly worried about her. Could she indeed withstand and sustain the difficulties and distress of the work? In her feeling that she should leave, she was experiencing a severe threat to her attachment bond to me. The hovering between holding on and letting go was intense. I did not fully have the language or even the clinical clarity at the time. What I did was stay close to her experience, feeling held myself by my supervisor who was able to provide the clarity and conceptualisation of what needed to happen, and what we were experiencing. He was very sure that the negative feelings were central to resolving the sense of crisis.

In supervision, we revisited the Winnicottian notion of the 'use of an object', an idea which supports therapists through the attacks that occur during the work (Winnicott, 1971). It is a unique opportunity for a patient/client, accompanied by their therapist, to experience something completely different in relation to their distress, rage, frustration and often overwhelming grief.

Following Winnicott, babies 'destroy' the object in their mind only to discover later that they have both survived. While Jane was relating to me as the 'good object' (better mother) she felt she omnipotently controlled me. I was her creation and she was forcing me to be 'her good mother', knowing that there was a part of this phantasy which was not real at all. She also believed that the 'bad' object had been or could be destroyed by her hatred. My survival, without retaliation, withdrawal or collapse, disturbs the magical thinking. The phantasy also extended to the idea that somehow she could go back and have the happy childhood with me in the role of the 'pretend mother', inevitably of course to let her down and disillusion her.

It was with the help and support of supervision that I could see how addicted she was to me and the therapy, in the way that it had been proceeding – 'little girl/better mother'. The painful material had always been split off and she was struggling more and more to keep it out of our relationship. The art therapy had come at a critical junction and provided her with some relief and a place to put out the primitive images.

The supervision provided me with the language to keep saying, in one way or another, something like: 'How important for you that someone can really be in touch with you when you feel so uncontained. Thus I can know and experience your distress when you feel uncontained and more significantly what it is like in my absences and when I am far away.'

The person in her mind would not have been able to allow, let alone welcome, her feelings about how she was being treated by them. In addition to her pain, there was also an intense and overpowering wish to punish the mother, who wasn't there for her and thus unable to be in touch with her as a child.

The challenge for the therapist is to remain calm and steady. But she did make it easier for me, in some ways, by confining the major and the most terrible attacking phantasies to paper. The letters enabled me to read them in my own time and to process them. Thus, by the time they came into the sessions, the worst of her phantasies had been already received and accepted for what they represented, communicated and meant. The letters, as already described, were indeed a most creative and helpful process – particularly to this aspect of the therapy.

Also, the letters highlighted the transferential elements in a way that it was no longer necessary for me to make a transferential interpretation to her at crucial points. I also felt that it was unnecessary to comment on the envious attacks she was making in the letter below.

> My pain goes from me to you and back again. How I wish I could have 'posted' my mother's rage and pain back to her – to where it belonged with her mother and hers and hers and hers. How hard to hold the accumulated pain of the generations in the scattered fragments of my mind ... I want to punish you for your health, your life, your peace, your family, your security, your ability to put me down when I am not with you, your lack of need of me.

This section of the work finally drew to an end. Throughout, as Jane worked to become more integrated and able to use her own mind, she continued functioning in the external world and in her other relationships, although still swinging between regressing into an early state of being and moving back into her grown-up self with me but becoming stronger and stronger. Gradually the conversations and the fighting about the 'little girl' ceased. There were probably times, even close to the finishing of the work, when she still connected internally to the 'little girl' but the spontaneous regressions ceased. The little girl seemed to have become integrated into the warm emotionally able adult that she was also becoming. And yet she continued, in the ordinary way in which many of us do, to remain in touch with a 'childlike' part of herself: a part that experiences the world with wonder and delight, as well as at times feeling shy or somewhat tentative or unrealistically angry or frustrated.

I will conclude this chapter with a brief statement about the overall process of the therapy. In the work with Jane, I provided a lengthy period of 'holding' which created a strong positive transference. It enabled Jane to trust that I was someone who had her best interests at heart unlike her experience when growing up with her parents. Consequently when we inevitably reached a stage in the work where it became important for her to experience and express her negative and angry feelings, in order to separate and resolve her dependency on me and the therapy, she had enough trust that I would not retaliate, collapse or withdraw. In that way she could truly begin a process to integrate me as a real person.

Chapter 5

Supervision
Finding the missing ingredient

Supervision has long been regarded as a necessary support for clinical work, throughout training and as a form of ongoing professional support. In the wide and diverse field of practitioners, experienced therapists make a variety of arrangements to support themselves: to provide space and opportunity to reflect on their practice and further their growth, and learning through the practice of regularly having supervision in one form or another, in what has now become a requirement of continuing professional development in this country.

To find a supervisor who is also a gifted teacher, practitioner and mentor, was one of the fortunate aspects of this work. By the time I found a new supervisor I knew that I was missing something essential in the work and had been unable to find the help I needed from my usual sources in the primarily humanistic and integrative field, respected peers and at times consulting experts. I needed to go beyond my own peer and colleague group. I was further fortunate in finding someone who was not only gifted, as described, but also flexible enough to work with me, even though I was not a practising psychoanalyst or trained as one.

The work with Patrick Casement, my new supervisor, began in the autumn of the third year some months before my long break. I had met with Patrick a few times when Jane started the art therapy. I took only this case, initially, to supervision and we focused on my transcribed sessional notes. We met weekly for a session and a half, so I was able to have ample supervision on each double session. This combination of changing supervisors, the intensity of the supervision and the encouragement that I was getting from someone I highly respected, soon began to impact dramatically on the work.

The impact of supervision

At the point when I started working with Patrick, in intensive supervision of this case, I had been feeling somewhat stuck and confused. I was worried as I didn't understand why my patient appeared to be either deteriorating or, at the very best, stuck and continuing in the same repetitive vein. Even though Jane, from her own point of view, was comfortable in the therapy and the way in which it was going, and others were noticing a difference, in the room with me I felt things were repetitive and stuck.

As already explained in previous chapters, the work was in the 'little girl/better mother' mode. Jane's letters at this time reinforced her perspective that this re-parenting process was what she needed, and how central the therapy and our work was to her.

In relation to me, Jane was perpetually regressed and this was one of my causes for concern. She would often arrive for sessions claiming to have got lost on the way. She looked pale and unwell with deep black rings under her eyes, and consistently presented in a regressed state, often speechless for a while at the beginning of sessions. During the course of the two-hour session she usually relapsed into a full-blown regressed state as a shy, albeit sweet, young child that I estimated was around the age of between four and seven.

I experienced myself being held (even trapped) in the role of a kind, loving, generous and permissive mother. I felt very controlled by Jane. She insisted that we sit near each other 'on the couch' in my consulting room, claiming to feel connected with me in this way with the couch as a concrete bridge between us.

The letters came very regularly as a sort of journal or diary, significantly providing me with a clear access to Jane's internal life. At this time we had a number of sessions in which we played being 'little girl/good mummy'. We went on phantasy journeys to a picnic, read young children's books, drew child-like pictures and even one day iced cookies that I had prepared for the session.

By now, late in the third year, the work and what she was writing in the regular letters to me had certainly moved on from the 'little girl/better mother' mode, and it contained much more ambivalence, conflict and distress. Jane continued to reassure me of the importance of the sessions what had been achieved, and she showed a powerful, strong, positive transference in spite of the negativity that was appearing in the correspondence. She was also clearly deeply attached to me. In some ways it seemed like a primary attachment, although the attachment style was both insecure and ambivalent.

Early on in the supervision, I was immediately attracted by Patrick's openness and flexibility. I knew of course that he didn't much hold with the model of a reparative experience (the 'corrective emotional experience'), the so-called re-parenting style of Transactional Analysis of the time. His style of supervision, rather than being critical, carried with it a flavour of being non-judgemental. He used to suggest other options or ways of making the intervention, with comments like: 'let's play with this', or 'another possibility may be to...'. This had the effect of opening up the learning and thinking in the supervision sessions. He combined this thoughtful, reflective process with at times sharing his associations, which were clinical and theoretical and always insightful. We shared the theoretical perspective of seeing early development as vital to the understanding of current internal processes, and we were both influenced by Winnicott's fundamental contributions to the field (Winnicott, 1982a, 1982b, 1971), with his stress on the significance of infancy to future development of emotional life.

In line with his own theories and contribution, Patrick was also constantly working with me to develop an 'internal supervisor', and would listen to the material as I reported it from the 'patient's point of view' (Casement, 1985). This perspective on my 'countertransference' proved to be invaluable, as feed-back on my style and clinical methodology, enabling me to understand what was being evoked in me and how I might be getting in the way of the work. In the light of a two-person, or relational psychology, it is obvious how valuable and enabling the supervision was. Further, I think that the results of the work confirm the validity of these comments and this perspective on the process of therapy.

Soon after I began working with Patrick, Jane said two things:

> I think the euphoria will soon fade, it doesn't seem natural. It is really my relief at being seen by you. I have been thinking about our early days of therapy and am glad that you didn't know then what you know now – either about me or in terms of what you think about therapy. You would not have agreed to take me on.

A bit later on she says 'I am so lucky to have found you', a sentiment I echoed in relation to the supervision.

Again, soon after understanding better what was not happening in the work, in an effort to evoke the 'negative feelings' in relation to me, I said something like: 'You might be very disappointed because we have now been working for a long time. If anything you are feeling no better and the work seems very far from coming to a conclusion.' Her response was:

> Yes, I am somewhat disappointed that it seems to be taking so long. However one thing I know about you is that when you don't know something you will make every effort to find out.

Patrick's comment on this statement was that it was a piece of 'unconscious' supervision, in that she had recognised a change in approach. In other words something had changed and was influencing the work (a 'new supervisor'). She also speaks at this time of her anxiety that I would be 'counselled out' of attending to her, presumably in the regressed mode of 'better mother/good little girl' that we had been working in.

In many ways it is difficult to sum up or quantify what I learnt through the supervision of this case from Patrick Casement. As I think about what he did that was so helpful to me, it was to help me translate my theoretical understanding of psychoanalytic ideas into their clinical implications, ideas that I had both read about and taught for years. However I was not a psychoanalyst, by training or exposure, and I had only known the ideas intellectually. My exposure, through being on the couch as a patient for a while, had been somewhat helpful personally, more intellectually than emotionally satisfying, but some of my own anxiety remained little changed.

As a therapist I was used to working much more actively and directly with the patient. I understood that this could be seen as 'acting out' something, role playing, or providing the 'corrective emotional experience'. On the other hand, a good deal of the TA/Gestalt approach, re-creating aspects of the past, identifying archaic beliefs and releasing affect through catharsis, were highly effective therapeutic ways of patients bringing about useful changes in their lives – sorting out crises and growing from the stresses and challenges that faced them.

The significant change to my work here was to acquire an understanding of how to work with unconscious processes, by integrating the psychoanalytic understandings with this more humanistic active and engaging way of working. These days I would go on to call this work 'relational' in frame, in line with the Relational Psychoanalysts, Relational Transactional Analysis and others. At the time of doing the therapy I had been reading Stephen Mitchell, Greenberg, Aron and their colleagues, and finding their ideas compatible with my own understanding (Mitchell, 1988; Greenberg & Mitchell, 1983; Mitchell & Aron, 1999). What was missing for me was a method of translating these insights into a meaningful dialogue with the patient. It is with this that I was most helped by Patrick, whose own work was familiar to me.

It seems to me that one of the ways of conveying the value of the supervision is by giving some flavour of Patrick's insights and how he would translate theoretical ideas into interventions. I was helped to understand that in my wish to be helpful I was often reassuring or being 'nice' rather than providing a presence in therapy for a client/patient to feel heard or not heard. The sort of comment that he helped me formulate would be something like: 'I think you are anxious about whether anyone could really be in touch with you when you feel so uncontained.'

Supervision and a changing view of the work

A moment in supervision: how the recovery of the boundaries was achieved

After some sessions of supervision, Patrick Casement said it was clear that we had to work towards recovering the boundaries. What was important was that we were building towards clearer boundaries as a response to the patient, not merely imposing them from a conceptual or theoretical stance.

He began by summarising what we had learnt about Jane thus:

> Jane seems to have developed a sense of herself as if she has a 'monster' in her mind, perhaps even of herself as a monster. What seems to have contributed to this view of herself has been her repeated experience of others not being able to manage the states of mind that she could not manage in herself. Others had been experienced as collapsing or as retaliating to her demands, her rages and her violence – real and imagined.

The art therapist had been presented with many images of Jane's internal world, but she too may have been experienced as collapsing in that she only engaged with the images as she had no mandate to work with them from the patient.

While I remained controlled by Jane, to be the 'better mother', I was protected from most of the 'monster' in her, as if I might have been destroyed by it. Instead, I was being subjected to an escalating demand for more good mothering, an almost addictive search for something Jane was not going to find. It would never have been enough for the demanding child in her.

I may also have unconsciously been afraid of becoming the monster, and only with the holding provided by the supervision could I become able to tolerate the attacks aimed directly at me.

So what was Jane needing?

As Patrick reviewed her behaviour with me, he made the point that much of her behaviour had been pointing towards what remained missing. She had never found someone who could really engage with *what she experienced as the worst in her*. And she could not find that in me (as the 'good Mummy') as I was being constantly protected from all of that.

Patrick went on to say: 'It was because of these multiple pointers, towards what she needed but was not yet finding, that I regarded this as a "gift" of unconscious supervision by the patient.' It all pointed to her need to find a strength in me that was not of her making. Until then she had kept me 'strong', by protecting me from any direct assaults of those unmanageable states of mind she had constantly been telling me about, primarily in the letters.

In response to these unconscious prompts, pointing to what she most needed to find in me, Patrick said: 'You have to assert yourself, and your own strength, beyond her former control of you.' This was the reason that I needed to move back into the 'analytic chair' and stop re-enacting the re-parenting.

He summed up this supervision thus:

> This move I am suggesting is, I believe, a needed response to the prompts in Jane's behaviour, and in her keeping the worst in herself outside of her relationship with you. It is not merely some analytic wisdom about boundaries. I think this is the only way that we can hope to meet Jane's unmet need: her need for genuine containment of that in her mind that has remained unmanageable – by her and by others.

Thus this supervision led to one of the most dramatic changes that I introduced into the therapy room. It arose directly as a consequence of thinking about the work from the psychoanalytic perspective and Patrick's capacity to see the problem and to help the therapist know what to do clinically, even in the integrative rather than psychoanalytic frame.

I changed our seating arrangements by moving off the couch. Immediately I felt less controlled by Jane and freer to think in the sessions. This of course had a major repercussion within the work and evoked an onslaught of protest, which was to continue unabated for a long time. There were many letters in this vein and some far more vigorous:

> Dare I send what I have written, that makes no sense ... I feel afraid. I have a sense that you want me to be sad and angry – to snatch away the 'good' mummy from the little people ... I can't write anymore.

The protests continued unabated for months and I took this question to Patrick. Jane felt very strongly that she needed the good experience that she didn't have for long enough in the therapy, and she was also strongly convinced that I was wrong to withdraw. Her doubts echoed my own questions about the therapeutic route now to be taken, and how to respond to her pleas for me to re-establish the 'good mother' experience for her.

I will address this question with an extract from my sessional notes and then the comments and discussion from the supervision session.

Sessional notes, 25 April

(This was in the spring of the fourth year, approximately six months after the beginning of the new supervision and the changed approach in my mind about the work.)

Unusually, Jane arrived 10 minutes late. I had started to feel anxious and checked the door a couple of times by the time she rang the bell.

She started off by saying: 'I am confused. I have had Ken Wright's book since 1993 [she is referring to Wright, 1991] *and I have not been able to read it. I started to read it on the train journey here, and got really confused and lost on the way here.'* By now I understood better that she was feeling internally regressed and possibly dissociated.

'And indeed I really needed to see you this week. To find you again.' She looks up directly at me and says: *'I can't read you...'* I was thinking that she was trying to read my face and find the *'lost self'* in it.

Slightly on in the session, referring to the previous session, I say: *'Things are confusing right now and between us.'* I continue with: *'I have read your last three letters [received since the last session] very carefully and the things you describe, surfacing in your mind, must feel very confusing. It is important for us to stay with your confusion.'*

I added something about our task needing to import the material from the art into our sessions and to make sense of it. I continued with: *'I am wondering what experiences, phantasies, things that you witnessed, or were exposed to, have left you with such an internal sense of disgust?'*

She responded by talking about her mother's looks of disgust and revulsion. *'You make me sick'*, she would say to her. As Jane remembers these scenes from her childhood she says she feels sick now. Then she herself made the link to Wright's book, talking about what he referred to as a *'look of revulsion'* and how this becomes internalised into the young child's sense of themselves.

Jane thus becomes able to bring into the room some of her awful images, describing her images of violence, wanting to smear my walls and attack me, sweep everything off the shelves. But there is a *'sentry'* patrolling in her head stopping her.

I had understood through my work in supervision that what was needed was to simply stay with her experience of being confused as well as recognise and refer to the disturbing material, which was now being expressed directly to me rather than through other channels. It was clear to me by now that the repetitive nature of these images of violence was somehow compelling and addictive.

In my notes from supervision I had said to Jane something like: *'I think it is important for me to allow you to stay with your experience rather than pre-empt you to make it better. You will re-find your loving connection in your own time. Furthermore you might be believing that I need you, or require you, to put aside your anger.'* (I may not have necessarily said this directly to her.) I was careful not *to become reassuring and thus send the message that I might not be able to take/bear her anger, thus falling into the same category as her mother. Falling into regression was one of her defences in relation to me. Reflecting her fear back, that something could be spoilt between us might leave no room for the hurt/needy child.*

At about this point in the work we were still arguing about one of our major disagreements, which precipitated a therapeutically induced crisis. I had moved across the room back to my chair and she was expressing her distress powerfully in all the letters, as well as verbally, directly to me. The pleading statements continued:

> I feel you moving away from them [the children in her mind], perhaps not knowing that they wait, staring mutely for a look, a touch, a word of recognition – they need some sign that you recognise that they are still there.

At the same time these words also refer to the split off and dissociated parts that we were now in constant conversation about. I was still exercised with how to bring the material that had appeared so vividly in her art therapy into our work together, and into the room between us. The essence of this work by now was also strongly in the letters from this time.

An irrevocable path to change

At the stage when the letters became increasingly violent and disturbed, in some sense becoming a bridge towards transporting the expression of primitive material from the art work into our work, I made the notes prior to a supervision session reflecting again my worry about removing the 'good mother' in her experience, as well as trying to understand the origins of the monstrous images.

Over and above the containing, ongoing insight and support, and the help with the unleashing of more and more negative material in my direction, supervision particularly enabled me to make sense of the most difficult expression of her primitive feelings – and the violence that was unleashed initially in the art therapy. This work proved, probably only in retrospect, to be at the centre of the healing for all the reasons developed below.

In many ways the disturbing material can be seen as having to do with 'unendurable agonies' (Winnicott, 1982a). When the pain and distress can't be contained, the child is left feeling that no-one can manage this and is thus thrust into an abyss of uncontainable feelings. Jane describes her internal experience in this way, giving vivid language to the 'unendurable agony'. First through painting, and now increasingly in words and in the letters, she found a way to let me know what her experience was and is:

> Waves of pain come over me – I'll burst in the rush to escape, be free – to do I know not what evil in the world. Demons, evil black, killing, maiming, torturing, glorying in blood, – hearing screaming of their still living victims ... The laugh rises from my belly, deep and black, spurious triumph for the 'good girl' the 'nice girl', kind, generous, loyal, loving. The devil from hell escapes into the world under no control, to add to the world's evil. Aligns herself with the putrifying, poisoning, cruel ... particularly to children.
>
> I frighten myself as I pour this out on paper. I could go on and on – wanting you to feel it too ... How did he [Winnicott] know it was unendurable? I need you to know the annihilating pain. I need you to 'hold' me. I am lost.

I have already discussed how helpful it was to keep bringing this confusing material to supervision, and working together with my supervisor, to read what she was saying about me as well as to me. What was emphasised, was that it was really important for me *not* to become reassuring but rather to give her the experience of being with someone who understands this fear, also being able to bear being in touch with it.

At this juncture Jane was keeping the material out of our sessions by writing about it, but she was also inviting me to treat her coping as not real. The danger would be that I could so easily slip into becoming reassuring at the expense of staying with the difficulties.

Jane is showing me that she is containing within herself very disturbing elements and what she needs from me now is to deal with them, rather than being afraid or deflecting from them. The question, where they come from, remained puzzling and it seemed important to find an answer to this. I endorsed the fact that this is an important question, and it might help her to make sense of her experiences of being taken over by these ideas and impulses.

In a letter at this time she says (in a letter already quoted above):

> This is an incredible, God-given opportunity to put something right, to heal the pain, to stake a claim for life, for happiness, for my future. I no longer fear – well not so acutely ... I do believe that you would recognise me on the street, remembering that I exist in the world.

The object permanence and a developing sense of trust in me that I had felt to be taking place over these months seems to have set in her, both about herself, me and our relationship. Jane carries on with:

> But it doesn't mean the 'little people' don't need the evidence that you see them ... About the safety of the setting the opportunity to connect with the craziness that has no words, I'm feeling a mixture of things.

She also says here:

> Perhaps this is the start of bringing the 'painting' me into the room – rush of energy – that means something is there. A new start? After the crisis...?

This continues with a summary of the supervision notes about this process, which of course is the beginning of the turning point and the way in which the change process is now irrevocably set in motion.

The good mother is there for the 'bad' experiences. The child worries that they, the 'little people', have to protect the mother from their feelings. Therapy provides the opportunity for the negative transference to deal with this. By becoming the representation of 'someone who can't be trusted', and making an intervention that sounds something like: 'in your mind I am someone who...'.

At this time I was also helped to find the words to say to Jane: 'I think what is happening between us at this moment is that you are experiencing me as impatient; as someone who expects too much from you; who has made too sudden a transition. Consequently you have become anxious that there is no space/room here for your "little girl" (vulnerable, sad and needy) feelings'.

I go on with:

> In writing to me you want to engage with the 'bad' mother so that we can get back to the 'good' mother. The phantasies contain rage and violence which need to be engaged with. I sense that you need to feel that I can sustain the firmness. You are nonetheless left with the worry that there is no space for the little girl. In the discovery that these expressions and experiences do not destroy me comes some security, rather than the mother's retreat from her child's legitimate needs and consequent rage at their neglect.

At this point in time Jane still experiences my firmness as a rebuff 'as if' I intend to provoke her. She is provoked by blanking off as she feels it to be so. I then say something like:

> I prefer you to bring me your feelings whatever they may be. Where there was no opportunity to find and express such feelings these turned into images instead. Thus you became tormented by images and you need to torment me with the feelings that have become images, which you also understand you can't cope with alone.

These are the notes made in the supervision:

Jane has a desperate need to communicate her intense feelings of hurt, but with an expectation that no-one can understand. The wish is to punish for not being willing to receive. If no-one is willing or able to receive her hurt it justifies her parents' inability to manage that hurt, since no-one else can, so how can they be expected to? Therefore they are not as bad as she fears they are.

There is also something eroticised in this material. The things are a mockery of what she wants and she finds this and then pushes for it. She needs me to know, and needs to know that another can know: that it is possible to be known by another. She is close to the point of recognition and the conscious hope that she can be understood.

Jane writes:

> I frighten myself as I allow this to pour out on to paper. I could go on and on – images, sensations, pushing to be revealed, known, felt, shared. Wanting you to feel it too, biting, tearing,

destroying. Keep out the good, with its agony, helplessness, its longing, yearning. Keep out the need, the jealousy, the terror of being dropped, overlooked, missed, not loved, not recognised, abandoned.

How did he [Winnicott] know that it is unendurable? [Jane repeats this from time to time as she tries to find words for her pain.] I need you to know the annihilating pain. I need you to 'hold' me. I'm lost, lost, lost. Less able to hold together. I need you to continue to 'hold' the hope. I shake and am weak like a kitten. Mad.

The essence of the madness and violence has made its way into our sessions and can now be processed between us.

Who is this baby? Who is the baby that she wants to smash up in the way she keeps describing? She needs a reconstruction that will be convincing enough to help her understand the 'monster' in her own child mind.

What comes to mind is the picture of a very unhappy young child who is desperate for the mother to leave the new baby alone. The slightly older small child hates the baby who takes the mother away. (Jane is in the middle of an older brother and younger sister, both of whom turned out to be violent and anti-social as adults.) Not only does she want to get rid of the baby at all costs, but also the hurt and pain she feels, by expressing it. The quality of the aggression is the measure of the hurt, and the less it is recognised the more violent the child becomes. What is needed is a setting in which to make sense of these feelings and this behaviour. These ideas were conveyed through statements of 'wondering ... not knowing if?'

Almost unwittingly, through the sequence of the art, the development of our relationship and the support of the supervision, a vein of unconscious phantasy had been stirred up and was seeking discharge. What is being picked up are extremes of psychological and emotional neglect, with echoes of perversion and sadism caused by the violence. It is as if Jane herself doesn't know much about this state of mind: what is excitement, disgust, and what it means to discover these extremes of feelings and associated images and the 'buzz' they create.

The images are putting feeling states into some communicable context, and eventually into words, both in letters and then directly in the room to me. In these states of mind Jane is back in an infantile state with the concomitant bodily sensations. These sensations are both repetitious and obsessive and she was gripped by them. What we have is a mixture between a temper tantrum and desperation. It is easy to become confused and make the same mistake as the mother. The tantrum is about my not giving her what she wants, whereas the quality of the desperation has to do with no-one understanding or gratifying her needs. If the desperation is treated as a tantrum we compound the problem, escalate the desperation and reinforce her belief that there is no-one who can understand her; and the 'monster' in her, that needs to be contained in the face of the escalating tantrum rather than succumbing to it.[1]

It is difficult to sum up the value and importance that the supervision had on the final outcome of the work. Not only was the transformational 'cure' life-changing for the patient, I too was changed personally and professionally by the understanding and growing. I was enabled to integrate knowledge and understanding about clinical process, and provided with what I would be inclined to call the 'missing link', from my own work but also from a humanistic approach to therapy.

Humanism based on Transactional Analysis, Gestalt Therapy and the more positive views of human nature, has a lot to offer as a philosophy and a frame to help people function better, to solve problems and relate to others. What the understanding of and developing the capacity to work with negative feelings, primitive states of mind, violence and aggression, enables humanistic practitioners to do is to provide opportunities for transformation. That clinical moving on from destructive forces to creative ones allows for the expression of the positive and loving features of our human potential to take charge.

Note

1 I will refer back to this point under the 'use of an object', one of the most important theoretical ideas to emerge through the supervision and the complex clinical presentation.

Chapter 6

The letters and their role in the therapy

Although the letters continued unabated throughout the course of the work, this chapter will concentrate on specific references to the letters in the letters themselves, as they took on a life of their own. In fact, they developed beyond being a channel of communication and connection into a particular vehicle through which the work of therapy was aided, as well as further enhanced and elaborated. Here too I lose the chronology by focusing on the specific content of the meaning of writing letters during intensive ongoing therapy for this patient.

This section will contain segments from some years before the work came gradually to an end and about half way after the full engagement of the work. Using fragments from the letters themselves is the most powerful and graphic way to show how they developed and what function they served. One of the 'gifts' in this work is in fact the patient's capacity to write from a number of points of view, the central one being how she is able not only to use words but to capture in them, and therefore open the window to, her internal experience and life.

The early letters have already been referred to in Chapter 2, some of the sequences giving a sense of their content, continuity and the 'flow'.

During the first sequence, half of the work, the majority of the letters were written with the voice of the 'little girl'. The tone of these early letters also captures something of the emotional quality of the therapy in the room. This state of the Ego, elaborated elsewhere, in many ways is the most predominant way in which she related to me. It was her internal state of regression, the part of her seeking the 'better mother', and that which had originally drawn her to me – seeing me as warm, wise and containing, as well as being able to understand her. For a large part of the work she held onto the phantasy that I would be her 'new mother', a mother of choice, and that if she were my 'little girl' she would grow up well and healthy.

> Working with the little girl is very disturbing ... I could keep on and on writing – I need to talk to you and this is the best way. I think she is going to be old enough for the pictures, too young for the story. She wants to burrow in your lap ... be rocked, held, sung to ... but you are far away and I can't hold her ... She wants her new mummy.

Although obviously she writes the letter as an adult, she is reporting on, or describing, her inner state in many of the letters, of which this is but a fragment – showing how close she is to these emotions and how able to capture the inner state, seeming to move between observing the child and being 'the child'.

In a typed letter the next day, reflecting herself on the use of the letters, Jane says:

> I have been thinking about the function of these letters – one of the things discussed was the degree to which clients censor material, especially material which may put them in a bad light, because as children this protected them from abuse. I think I have consistently done that in other therapies. The difference with you started with the letters. When I started writing the letters I wrote to someone I never saw, so in a way it was safe, and for a long time the sense of unreality persisted and my letters still went to some other 'Diana'. It somehow opened up a way of communicating, of being honest, which is still often frightening because of the times when I reveal too much and get a terrible backlash, but which is often a joy. I feel really connected with you at the moment.

A month or so later Jane speaks about her wish to censor what she has written. This letter shows how she is more able to think and notice what she is writing to me.

> Of course now I feel tremendously embarrassed and can't decide whether to delete what I have just written – but on the principle that it is important not to censor myself in these letters

> I decide not to do that. It is such a humiliating need for a woman my age to need a Mummy so much. I feel that with a 'real' mummy I can stop searching, stop living out the consequences. In fact as I write this I feel that sense of joy at having found you and at last feeling that there is a place for me, that I belong. I think writing this at this time is a displacement activity ... it is much nicer to write to you than do anything else.

A few weeks later in a second letter written that day, Jane shows another, different and more consistent use of the writing for her.

> I need to write again. I really feel internally very 'wobbly' and very frightened. I just feel I need to keep making contact with you, and the way I do that is to write. This is equivalent of talking to you several times a day. It's true that my connection with you is the same as my connection with life – you are at my centre.
>
> I am thinking about these letters – of their function in keeping my connection with you, of the intimacy.

Several weeks later the post-session letter shows how she has been able to process the session. These post-session letters proved to be helpful in several ways. She had by now got into the pattern of leaving her double session, going into a coffee shop for breakfast but also writing almost immediately after the session ended. This allowed her to carry on working, and to say some of the things she hadn't been able to say or had only thought about in the session, as well as continuing to process the session. This processing of course would often continue into the next day, as this fragment shows:

> A tremendous need to write to you. Yesterday's session left me in a turmoil – and I feel the need to pour it out. I realise that I keep the rageful, destructive, angry self away from you because I need the loving connection with you so much. I am very frightened that my rage would destroy your good will, your love and there is no time to work with that. How can I be in such a position of conflict when I rely on you so? You may feel you have made a mistake.
>
> I feel in a 'state'. Of course at one level I know about the 'split' – though I hadn't really thought about it until you talked about it. I have always operated that with you – for a long, long

> time the Diana that I wrote to had no connection with the Diana that I saw in London and that Diana had little connection with the Diana I saw elsewhere in the world. Mostly now I write to the Diana that I see.

Now she is able to see and describe her awareness of the value to her psychologically, in keeping the splitting operative and thus solving the dilemma of the feared consequences of her rage and anger with me, while at the same time needing my good will so desperately.

Some days later she says:

> One day it will be important to go through some of the letters with you – not now. I almost need a therapy about the pain of the therapy.

One of the clinical problems was going to be integrating the material from the art therapy into our work together, as discussed in the outline of the work above. The art work had allowed for the unleashing of the primitive, 'psychotic' aspects, which had been so heavily defended against and early repressed, as well as dissociated from, to blossom in full flow. As will be seen in the discussion of the art work above, naturally she was able to split the two therapists and therapies, for a while, keeping her 'therapist' good, kind and loving, while being more able to use the 'art therapist' as a representation of some of the negative feelings she had towards authority figures and 'parent-like' relationships. Quite quickly it became apparent to me that in the art work she was able to express even more graphically the abandonment, hatred and attacks, that my recurring absence provoked for her. Consequently, this material also surfaces in language, particularly in the letters she wrote to me at that time, and then finally face to face in the sessions. Thus the letters and the art work together provided the bridge for integrating the 'good' and the 'bad' object and also the 'good' and the 'bad' child. Furthermore this shows one of the ways in which she used the art therapy, as well as the other forms of 'holding' experiences of therapy during the breaks in our work.

Through the letters, Jane, suffering from early abandonment and rejection, had found a way of satisfying her need for ongoing connection and closeness with her therapist, which would otherwise have taken analysis four or five times a week to achieve. These letters seem to provide her with the sense of continuity and help through the 'state of absolute dependency' (Winnicott, 1982b).

Then in the next letter, a different experience, she also comments on how it doesn't always solve the problem:

> I so wish I could ring you to ground myself. Writing is one thing but it doesn't re-establish the connection between us.

Thus sometimes writing works, to bridge the spaces between sessions and the feelings of abandonment, and sometimes it doesn't.

The change in approach and therapy as reflected in the letters

The next set of extracts come from the spring of the following year. A lot had happened. I had been away for a break in the winter. This year there was no substitute therapist. I had negotiated, with the help of my supervisor Patrick Casement, properly bounded and agreed-on sessions by phone with my patient. They were 50-minute sessions at an agreed day and time and treated as appropriately paid for sessional time. There was very little correspondence until my return to London. I pick up the correspondence here again with particular reference to her use of the letters to me while we were also meeting regularly.

In this particular letter Jane vividly describes some of her internal experience of dissociated states, captured in clear images that make sense to her but also to me. She was only later able to use these descriptions in sessions with me. Thus the communication via the writing formed a bridge to her being able to conceptualise and describe her inner world.

> 18th April
> A need to write. I am so afraid that you will lose touch with the other 'versions' of me. At the moment I feel steady, in coping mode, well functioning ... I am so scared that you will see this 'coping' self as all of me – You are the one who sees, knows, touches, allows the vision of the grey baby, so near to death, the pink baby who grew in response to you, the wide eyed trusting little girl who in her shyness felt the delight of her Mummy's protection and love ... they need some sign that you recognise they are still there.

And two days later a consciously stated wish to use the letters to keep things out of the session.

> I don't know – next time you see me I may be spitting venom again. I am writing all this stuff, I realise, to get it out of the way and keep it out of our session on Thursday. I want to keep your room protected.

At this time I made this observation: it seemed to me that the letters had become part of the enactment of connection and abandonment. I was troubled on an ongoing basis by the times when I was away, especially the longer gaps. It was not as if, however, the internal work went on hold during that time. Although I think she too worried hugely about the gaps, and somehow believed that she needed to physically see me for the work to continue: this was and was not true.

Of course, a certain amount of regularity provided her with the reality of our relationship. However there was a way in which we were both protected by the space. Most significantly I think the ongoing enactment of connection and abandonment was central in some way to the internal process, and the letters provided the container for the madness which surfaced in my absences – to be dumped into and disposed of. The gaps were often triggers for the distress and fury of abandonment. We had therefore created consciously, but also powerfully unconsciously, the real experience of my abandonment. Thus also on my return, the vehicle created through the letters, enabled her to continue to communicate these feelings directly to me – with some sense that I was receptive to them and was being impacted emotionally by her.

> What can I write that doesn't sound like a litany of complaints – it's like not being able to paint. Can't draw, can't convey what is going on. It doesn't read on the page how it feels inside. It reads like moaning and complaining, whinging and carping ...
>
> Another change to fear. Dare I send what I have written, that makes no sense ... I can't write any more – as every time I try sleepiness overtakes me.

And then the next day:

> Compulsion to write, urgency to put feelings and thoughts on paper. Probably repetitive but necessary ... I need you to not be

> scared, not to pull back, when the craziness is there. I need to paint its ugliness, its gore, its dismembered parts. Maggots ... It's another world of green and black. I feel like vomiting now – I have to come back. – I want to stay longer with my images ... Diana don't abandon me in this mad place.

She now begins to find words and language to describe the intense and mad images that she has as she experiences the powerful and primitive feelings of rage, and destructiveness, through her wish to attack and destroy the source (me) of her perceived and experienced distress. In the letters she describes the intensity and physicality of the pain she experiences. She also expresses her need to get me to understand the desperation she feels, particularly as she senses my withdrawal from being 'the good mother'. These 'longing, yearning internal child states' are further compounded by jealousy and rage, at the thought of me with 'sibling' like figures, that she may know of.

The power and creative use at this stage of the work is that she can now use the channel of communication, the letters, which has been established between us, to capture her internal experience in language as opposed to the images which she used during the art work. Thus the expression of these disturbing, unacceptable and dangerous wishes remains and they are kept safely on paper. At the same time they are also still accessible to expression, making them understandable as well as allowing them to be processed and integrated rather than split off, dissociated and unconscious.

> I am capable of destroying the therapy and that frightens me. It's as though a part of me wants you to say you have gone too far, want too much and that I'll be sent away. Part of me is utterly gleeful – doesn't want the 'little people' to grow healthy and strong. Hates it when they feel connected and loved. Wants to kill me, wants to kill you. Part of me comes with the intent to destroy. I need you to know, be wary, see.

Continuing to capture these themes, in a second letter, written post-session a few days later, Jane now describes another and far more vicious split-off state, saying:

> I have just this minute put the other letter in the box and feel overwhelmed by my need to write to you again. This time it's

> not the 'devil's child' but the terrible yearning. My neediness feels overwhelming ... You punish the little girl and the babies by refusing to hold them, give them time, even acknowledge their existence – perhaps not their existence but their presence. If anyone needs punishing it's the 'devil's child'.

It occurred to me that it was likely, in the past, that someone in her family, mother or grandmother (or Jane herself), had been called or thought about themselves as the 'devil's child'.

At about this time Jane was still dealing with the dramatic shift I had made by sitting across the room from her, and in a way this move seems to have precipitated the 'madness'.

A third letter followed the one above, even more disturbing and replete with descriptions and images of disgusting nature, flesh rotting, filth, etc., with her enjoying and embedding herself in it. She ends this third letter with:

> Eating, grubbing ... Perhaps I need to stop this. Stop talking, stop writing, put the 'devil-child' away. This can't be good or helpful. I will stop. Telling you is a form of abuse. I want you to be sickened by me.

In the same way as a lot of this material was dissociated from her ordinary conscious states of mind, so too I read the letters without being too disturbed. On the contrary I was puzzled and unsure about how to interpret them or make sense of them. I hardly ever mentioned them in sessions, while at the same time indicating that I received and read them as they arrived.

It seemed that what was important was that Jane should be free to write whatever she needed to. Further, I think now that she was finally managing to put into words what had splashed out with the art therapist. This material had caused the art therapist a lot of concern at the time. At last it was being directed to me, at me and about me, allowing the integration to occur in her therapy.

'The healing connection'

The next day Jane says it, showing how she regards the letters as a 'healing connection'. I have already said I was seeing them as a form of a diary or journal about her inner state, during the course of the work. I also conceptualised them as milestones or way-marks on the path to wholeness and health, providing a safe and contained space within which to share her experience without having to manage my response.

Now we reached a point in which she felt her reality has been accepted. She also feels herself changing. I was of course encouraged by these signs of changes, beyond the confusion and anxiety that I experienced reading her disturbed flow of consciousness.

> I'm feeling blank – nothing to say, feeling nothing except a need to spin a fragile connection with you.

This raises a significant and important question about an analytic way of being with a patient. At this time I was truly confused. I was deeply worried by the 'acting out', what Patrick Casement called 'role playing'/'better mother'/child interactions.

I feel on firmer ground with what I would label an 'integrative, relational' approach. Thus, although I would not go too far down the road of the 'better mother' approach, nonetheless this case gives me strong evidence for the acceptance of the powerful transferential projection and the reparative effects of an unchallenged 'holding' for a period in the work (Slochower, 1996).

Here are her dramatic and clear words about her experience in therapy and the strong need she had – and at this stage still experiences – to be met on multiple levels. She talks in this fragment of 'your warm heart and your fine mind': surely, if anything, a call for an integration of both within a therapist.

The inevitable change as seen through her letters to me

These extracts from the letters are now presented sequentially, tracking the changes as they are happening and as she is conveying them to me over the course of the sessions, both before and after them.

> I am scared others will counsel you out of honouring my complexity ... I'm scared of the change in you, the change in your style – scared that you will retreat behind an analytic mask and I will lose you forever ... I would not be able to do that if you didn't reach out for the little ones. I feel bereft. Cast out ... I

> know you don't want me to but I need the loving connection. I need your warm heart as well as your fine mind. The little girl thinks you don't like her any more ... I deliberately did not choose the purely analytic model of therapy ... because I knew it would send me crazy ... because I need someone 'real' to hold on to, relate to, to represent the external world ... In fact what I think is happening is that I am with you more able to find the lost ones. Lost in their psychoses – untouched, unseen, closed eyes bandaged faces ... jostling, pushing like a disorderly queue – all impatient to meet you, be seen.

This letter confirms something about how these various dissociated parts have surfaced into her consciousness, and how she has now developed a channel to communicate them to me, thus creating the way for their integration and slipping into memory. This shift, rather than arising to 'torment her when she begins to feel unmanageable feelings and experiences', leaving her in the grip of those dissociated parts in a seemingly uncontrolled way, is working in the service of integration. Almost as if these 'states of being' have now been unleashed into consciousness, clamouring for expression as she has lifted the lid that was on them, and she can no longer control what she experiences.

> All I am saying is that I need you in this process with your acceptance, warmth and love as well as the rest.

Thus the letters were used to capture – from the mists of repression – memories, perhaps 'felt memories' of the dissociated past, as well as good experience. She needs to do this work in the 'presence of another' as it can't be done alone. That was the problem in the first place. The child's experience of being left alone with unmanageable feelings, tormented internally, and in relationship with significant others (parents) who are supposed to be the containers and regulators of overwhelming experience, internal and interpersonal.

Catching what is in between the cracks

> Maybe that is really the function of the letters – to capture the moment – so that you know, so the moments are not lost, as so much else is lost in my memory ... Feels like so much falls

between the 'cracks'. This letter is a container of joy, of bliss, of quiet, peace, satisfaction and hope.

It took such a long time for Jane to be able to 'trust' me. I remember how surprised I was when she said around this time in a session: 'I am now really beginning to trust you', meaning of course what she writes here. Also, here is an important comment to therapists not to be too active about 'changing' someone or something. We can't do that. Only the other can change themselves, otherwise it is an adaptation to the therapist.

> My third attempt to write today. I think I would like to see you every day, but once a week is as much as I can manage. The work is so disturbing ... And takes so much from me that I need a break ... I can talk to you – I have amazed myself at my level of trust in you – I really am trusting you to know, to hold, to understand to help me stay safe, to contain. I don't want to be changed but held and understood, so that I can be the one who changes.

And then comes a mad letter saying all the unsayable, rageful attacking hatred. What follows are snatches illustrating the myriad of changing inner experiences of herself. By now I was seeing these therapeutically constructed letters as her lifeline to health.

> There is someone laughing a terrible evil laugh. Laughing at you, at me ... now I'd like to gouge your eyes out while you scream for mercy ... Stop meddling – play with the babies – leave us alone. Go Go. You don't know what you get into.

And the next day after three contrasting, distressed and confused, letters from some of these differing states of mind:

> A painful need to write ... I continue to write because as I form the words on the page I feel a connection to you ... I live with fragments, shards of glass. I feel so lonely and ashamed – actually not so ashamed anymore – something in my contact with you that is helping me to be less ashamed and secret and take myself seriously ... The writing has helped.

What is becoming much clearer half way through this penultimate year is that, with the trust Jane is also sharing with me, there is a deeper meaning of the ongoing correspondence for her and between us.

At the time it wasn't so obvious that the change process was now unstoppable. We still were to go through some scary moments, crises and points at which the therapy could have broken down, but at this stage I was now well established in a supervision that held me through the uncertainty and confusion of some of the psychotic material.

> What you did in those months was to allow the connection, allow the letters, allow phone calls, take my need seriously, tell me we would be together and work it out. I think if you had been scared off and withdrawn then – I really would have broken down – though at last I believe you will not do this to me –

The letter that follows came after a session in which, from my sessional notes, I said something to her about her experience with me of being held and then abandoned. She talks about my trips to South Africa at the end of the year (this is still six months away as these sequences come from July). In the conversation, I agree that this is cruel to the 'little girl', very cruel to send a three-year-old away, who can't understand what is happening.

I had made a note in supervision about the importance of being around for the feeling rather than trying to soothe it. Being around without collapsing, retaliating or abandoning, while I am now, with the support of supervision, working towards extracting myself from the role of the good mother and accepting that of the 'failing mother', as discussed more fully in 'The Use of an Object', below.

> 7.30 am and already my second letter. I don't know what I need to say, just hope that writing will release some of the pain ... you inflict pain in the name of healing and then tell me it is good for me, that the agony means we are always working on the edge. That the absences help the process –

Quality of 'self-soothing'

And the fourth letter written on that day. In this one we see the 'self-soothing' aspect of the letters and what relief they bring at times:

> I can't stop writing, this letter is an attempt to quieten my brain in the hope that I might sleep. Since my last letter – I am now in bed – It is very late. I need to tell you that despite the pain and anger the little girl has snuggled happily for the night with her thumb in her mouth.

And then more clarity, as she deals with the multiple and complex relationship she has in her mind with me:

> ... writing does not help ... I am glad you let me write – but I need human beings as well. I know from experience that this pain will pass. I will click into stop feeling – but for now it is terrible. The little girl is delirious with pain ... She longs for the 'old' Diana back – not this imposter who is so cold to her.

And then in the next letter:

> I am so afraid she will do what I did as a child – look for other people's mummies to be kind grown-ups.

In a post-session letter some weeks later, these positive signs are appearing in spite of much distress, anxiety and pain:

> I have not 'processed' our meeting today, and this letter is a 'want' rather than a 'need' to write to you ... What I notice is a lightening of my heart and – unbidden – a small bubble of hope. Hope for what? I don't know.

And now a sign of a new kind of Object Permanence as well as the recognition that I have my own and separate mind:

> What I think is – despite the disruptions, the process continues – because we have 2 hours at a time. Also – I continue 'working' in between and the letters are a big part of that ... I am having a sense of you over time – I can smile when I think of you.

And in another letter about a month later:

> My energy is with the therapy – my hope for the future.

Insights are coming more and more frequently (penultimate year of the work):

> I know that the early part of the sessions is always difficult for me, and I do regress, get paranoid, project.

Another indication of the changes occurring and how these are reflected in the letters as a barometer of our relationship (a month later):

> Time passes, operating in competent 'professional' mode – but still the stirrings of something important that I want to say. I found myself musing on how come I wrote so little in the time you were away. It wasn't because you were not at home to read the letters – this made no difference to me in the past. It was because for the first time – I have a choice. Up until now writing has been a compulsion – no sense of appropriateness, rightness, limiting the quantity – only at the physiological level the need to write. Now I have a choice (sometimes) it's more complicated. I am not responding to the internal 'rush' of energy. So I can feel angry and not write – a kind of 'sod you – who needs you anyway'.

The beginning of the ending: swinging between madness and sanity/clarity

We began to move into the beginning of the ending. Even though the letters were still repeating some of the early themes – showing the violent, primitive and disgusting material – they continue to move towards an ever greater conscious understanding of herself: how she is using writing to me and how the therapy is developing towards greater integration and health.

Further, the letters now also deal with some of our early history and previous enactments between us. Jane talks about the difficulty, re-traumatisation and repetition in the transference of her experience with her mother, in the early days of our work together, being able to tell me about the experience in a way that was impossible before. She probably didn't herself fully understand why it was so painful, but she would also have been too scared to voice such negative or distressed feelings.

Clearly there was enough difference, and positive helpful experience, for the therapy to have survived this early phase. Now there was also enough 'trust' or sense of security with me for Jane to be able, albeit in a letter, to communicate the real way in which she experienced me failing to understand what she needed from me, and the real pain and distress caused, although the difficulty could also be seen as a transference re-enactment. I could now take responsibility for my lack of attuned responses and hear the pain, bear being a 'failing' therapist at that time, without being defensive, attacking or denying her experience.

This letter is a good example of how some of the building blocks towards the 'use of an object' were put in place:

> I need to write because waves of pain are interfering with me. I am not sure why everything I read throws me back into the painful memories of our relationship ... I keep having 'flashbacks' to the pain of our beginning – to when I realise how I fell into breakdown. The horror of that, of meeting you, of you reaching out to touch me, of the long, long separation ... of the lurching connectedness followed by the sickening thud, agony of abandonment ... Of needing you to understand – you seemed to grasp it – then you would do something which made it obvious I had failed to communicate my desperation. I feel sick, sick ... Your irritation at my clinging, my clinging was a way of keeping my slim hold on sanity. The terrible circle I remember well with my mother ... I can't bear the memories – of you, of her.

Now a post-session letter, which is one of the most psychotic to date even though this was now late in the work and Jane had acquired a good deal of understanding of the nature of our relationship, particularly the early transferential projections:

> I keep seeing you sitting smugly in your chair – far away from me – taunting me, humiliating me with your power. How can you do this to me (I wanted to write how dare you do this to me). – enjoying, glorying in my pain ... I feel like killing you – ripping your head off, tearing you apart – smearing your blood and guts all over your neatly ordered room, your nice chair. That will teach you not to torture me.

Jane carries on in this vein, elaborating on her phantasies of torture, inflicting pain and torment, as a way to get me to understand her psychological experience of being tormented, tortured, ground into the dust by the humiliation she experienced at my hands, in her mind.

I made a note here, about wondering whether babies have phantasies of devouring the mother, particularly in the face of deprivation and continually experiencing abandonment, as suggested by Melanie Klein's views of early hatred and Winnicott's 'cupboard love' (remembering that he was supervised by Klein; see Segal, 1981; Likierman, 2001; Winnicott, 1971, 1982a).

> I need someone to help me soothe ... I've been pretending I am sane, it's not real ... I must stop – writing makes me crazy.

Then a second letter follows, suggesting that I am now calculating and cruel, followed then by this:

> I feel terrible – I've just written a terrible letter – and I am sorry. It seems that all the nastiest parts of me are bursting out, the calculatedly cruel sadistic parts of me – and I am feeling ashamed, guilty. I need you to know that what I write is real – and that somewhere else I know that at last I am getting the help I've always needed.

In this letter Jane is able to describe to me how she is expressing aspects of her real experience and how critical this communication to me is to her.

> ... help to show and be and reveal unmentionable, unspeakable, cruel, chaotic, sadistic, psychotic parts. I have been 'good' ... all my life and have always known about the others ... as long as you were being wonderfully loving and kind to me – all that stuff stayed hidden or poured out on paper in words or paint ... I am sorry if you are bruised and bashed ... but what I write comes from my deepest soul and is also an authentic part of me. I also need you to know of the deep gratitude and love and awareness I have about how hard working-in-this-way is for both of us. I still love you in my very being and hate and want to destroy you at the same depth. I won't censor my letters – I need to pour the poison out ... Your love built the foundation of trust in your goodwill – so

> that I dare do what I am doing ... I need to write because I am pretty sure that I will not be able to hold this perspective all the time ... I feel better having put the record straight, maybe I can relax and afford not to write for a while.

She follows this with a letter full of disgusting images, descriptions of torturing and pain. As she attempts to make tangible the unspeakable distress that she feels, the sense that she is being played with and that I am actively and sadistically the agent and the cause of her pain. It becomes clearer and clearer to me how the letters are now functioning between us. So I sit with her in the room knowing about this 'monster' inside, these views also of me, while at the same time we continue to have ordinary therapy conversations. She also, in this piece, shows how her mind searches for an explanation for my perceived cruelty to her.

The reference to the 'Holocaust' is often used, in my experience in Europe, even where there are no direct links, by patients as an image of extreme cruelty. She refers here again to my Jewishness but she had no conscious knowledge of any more immediate connection that I have to this massive tragedy.

> I can't stop writing – I feel so bad – I want to hurt you, hurt you ... I want to disgust and offend you – I want to degrade and torture you ... I want you to beg, crawl, squirm, plead – just like you make me do ... how can you live with your current cruelty to me ... I don't care if this sounds mad – maybe I am.
>
> Why does she need a sacrificial victim? I know her people were terrible victims – maybe I am being called upon to pay the price.

In a brief line or two she emphasises how thoughtful and aware she is that the letters arrive on time and that they are read:

> I write rubbish but need to keep the sense of contact that writing brings. I have run out of 1st class stamps so I don't know when you will get this.

And then her words about the lifesaving aspect of the letters:

> I imagine you reading my letters and shrugging. You allow them – and for that I am deeply grateful – I could not manage this therapy else.

The multiple uses but always a road to health

Some of the letters of course were highly disturbing. The revulsion she mentions is hers rather than mine. I knew well by now the significance of the letters to her and the work. I was pleased that Jane had found a way of communicating the internal turmoil and yet keep us both safe. My goal of integrating the art therapy had now been well achieved. Finally and importantly we were able to be together with her knowing that I knew about all this internal, and hitherto inaccessible, side to our relationship. I was also, on an ongoing basis, getting feedback about myself and how things were developing.

> The letters – I think I've understood that they are often (not always) the equivalent of the paintings, and as such, part of the therapy. What I don't know is how that works. The letters are what happens to me when you are not there – it's hard to know or access those feelings/thoughts in your presence ... I guess another way is to physically bring the letters into the sessions – if they are relevant in any way. It's not that I don't remember writing. I know I write. I do remember the content of some – like this one. The letters have different functions. This one is about me trying to work/sort something out – and to relieve some agitation. Some 'pour out' of pain induced or madness – some start one thing and become another. It's the ones that 'pour' which I can least hold on to. I guess these are the ones to which you refer – that you would like to return unopened. I felt your anger and revulsion as you said that.
>
> The more I write the worse I start to feel so I'm needing to stop. I think I am connecting with something beneath my frantic attempts to think logically ... time and again I bob and weave, trick and slide, slip away, confuse confabulate, lie and cheat ... I am lost. I lose myself – lose you ... It's like dealing with a bunch of anti-socials.

And then she says, remarkably:

> – there are many levels of need, many reasons for writing and writing helps me with staying sane and with going mad – both of which appear to be essential ... There is a part of me that wants to do terrible damage, to rip, tear, bite – consume you ... I am scared now to give myself up on paper. If I give up

> pouring without controlling what I do then he (the male alter) goes ... How can you know the pain which is hidden behind her terrible images and words which overwhelm you with violence.
>
> How can I know her, give her a voice without damaging you and thus our connection? The paper is the safest place in the world. I so wish I could 'pour' into notebooks, into poems, into some form of writing which did not have to be so directly in contact with you.
>
> I wish writing were enough, but writing is only half the story – the other half is posting, reading – imaging and knowing that my heart is connected to your heart in the deepest, darkest most terrible, vile awfulness. I both do and don't want to hurt you. I do and don't want you to survive, untouched, unmarked, unhurt, unaffected by what I write – and yet to be affected enough that you 'know'.

Jane's thoughts had been thought about in this way in supervision: the significance is that she can be with me while knowing that I know about these wishes and images.

In Winnicott's (1971) 'Use of an Object', he describes and explains this phenomenon of wanting to rage, bite and destroy while at the same time needing to feel held, understood and contained. As he describes, the infant can smash, tear, bite, rip, destroy the mother in its mind and the mother survives unscathed allowing the infant to begin knowing that she is separate from him, has her own mind and is beyond his omnipotence.

> ... the letters. A wonderful, painful release – but then I must write, write, write – some attempt to give voice to the voiceless, form to the formless, reach out across the page. I am not a writer, this is not my gift, I wish it were, that writing would be enough, that once written there would be no need for the folding, the envelope, your name, the stamp and the final release of the post box. I wish I didn't need your eyes, your mind, your heart. I wish I could 'pour' it into a journal and lock it up and keep it safe ... This sounds like a crazy lover – I am so grateful for the walls, the door, the day, the time, the appointment, the money. Grateful for the gaps, your family, your friends ... they form an impenetrable barrier between us and keep you safe ... It is often naked in

the letters, raw, open, weeping and bloody. But it can't escape the lines of ink on paper, sealed in an envelope and miles away.

Here is another passionate statement about the letters, that they are read, seen and part of our relationship.

What I think was important as well, was that they were never read together in a session. I never really held her to account, demanded explanations. Yet I can see how central they were to her and to our relationship, and her need of a relationship.

This chapter has specifically drawn from, and focused on, how Jane wrote about the function the letters were serving over the years of the work. It illustrates the way this changed and also the variety of functions that the letters served, both in her inner life as well as a behaviour that contained the waves of anxiety and agitation that she often felt.

The sessions themselves and the direct contact between us always evoked strong emotional responses. Clearly the 'post-session' letters that were almost always written after leaving therapy, and on her journey home on the train, are the best examples of how the processing of therapeutic encounters and experience continues in the mind.

Chapter 7

Finishing the work
The final crisis and ending

How does one bring such a long and complex story to a conclusion? The almost fairy tale finish was just about more than one could have wished for. Jane's goals were to become less continually anxious, less self-conscious and so easily filled with shame and embarrassment. My goals were to free her from the raft of problems that she carried, to liberate the dissociated parts and in short let her find and become herself.

When she started therapy with me, Jane indicated persecutory and delusional views of herself and how others saw and experienced her. She lacked the mirroring of an adult and competent self. In her mind, her family would have thought of her as the awkward, and difficult to relate to, child or at the worst moments as a 'devil's' child. I speculated that her mother could have projected some of her split views of herself, including the 'devil's child', onto Jane. This name ('the devil's child') was Jane's term for the dissociated part that contained the worst of the monster that she felt herself to be.

Jane's perception of her first husband's view of her was that he had long lost any positive feeling for her, probably swinging from seeing her as a nuisance and interference to his life to a burden and responsibility who needed to be got rid of. Similarly she felt her friends and colleagues, were ambivalent about her. Those with positive and loving feelings for her were unable to counteract Jane's overall feelings of inadequacy, unlovability and self-loathing that she carried around about herself most of the time. I saw her initially as an extremely stressed, uncertain and anxious person who lacked confidence in herself and felt herself to be vulnerable and sensitive to others' views of her acceptability or otherwise.

Against this relational background, what was to emerge once most of her transferential feelings towards me were resolved, was a woman becoming able to achieve a loving relationship with a suitable man that was reciprocated, fulfilling and sustainable. This was a fitting conclusion to the long intense relational work and great struggles we had engaged in, to create an intimate relationship within which she came to know herself and to be herself: to find her capacity to become the loving, generous and extremely able person that she was capable of being. Once we had turned the corner, and reached the depths of her distress towards completing a fourth year of therapy, Jane began to move rapidly towards cutting down on her sessions and eventually over the final eighteen months seeing me for a once or twice a year check-up.

About two years after we formally finished, when it was clear that the work was complete, we met for several hours in a neutral place so that we could reflect together on what had happened, what had been achieved and what if anything we would do with reporting on the work.

We needed to consider how to capture some of what had been written in the letters and how to bring our long, close therapeutic work to an end. In this meeting we both recognised the value of reporting and publishing aspects of the therapy, as an aid and inspiration to others and for professionals engaged in this gratifying but complex work.

However, before achieving this ending we had to negotiate a number of crises of confidence, and a not unexpected wish to end prematurely rather than confront the meaning of our finishing the work and Jane's long reliance on me – both in reality and in her inner world. It meant giving up phantasies, wishes, and projections that had become life-sustaining for most of her life.

Final crisis

In retrospect it became obvious that the change was now not only irrevocable but also the long process of therapy was coming to an end. I have called this section the 'Final crisis', because we had by this time survived a number of crises and challenges to the viability of the work often with the spectre of rupture hanging over us. Several months before my annual departure in the last year of our regular meetings, Jane had separated from her first husband and moved out of the marital home. During this stressful move she suddenly announced that she wished to cut back on her sessions citing for the first time the cost, affordability and expense of the therapy.

Quoting my sessional notes in this regard:

After a long explanation of the expense and difficulty of the journey involved in coming weekly to London, Jane said she wanted to cut back her sessions. She thought I would be pleased and relieved to hear this.

I commented that I was pleased she was feeling better but nonetheless felt it was a strange time to cut back. At this comment she got visibly upset and said: 'When you are here I don't need you and when you are gone I want you.'

When she made this comment, I thought about my absences and the gaps in the work in a different light. The absences, while causing stress and strain in one way also served the valuable function of preserving distance and space. Throughout the work Jane had been negotiating a process of separation and individuation from me, thus needing to manage the contradictory pressures and pulls of the 'fear of abandonment' versus the 'fear of engulfment'.

After this difficult conversation between us Jane suddenly became little, regressing, and said: 'the little girl wants to put her head in your lap. How do you respond to her?'

In the letter following this session Jane said:

> ... it doesn't make sense that you resist me quietly slipping away. I feel this is what I need to do – quietly without fuss – just erase myself from life. Suicide is too strong a word – with images of drama, pain, loss, violence, anger – I just want to gradually become invisible – so imperceptible that no-one notices. My children are the flies in the ointment – everyone else would carry on seamlessly. Your life, your consciousness, your enjoyment, your happiness would not even register – I would be a faint memory – like a trace of perfume or the edges of a dream that cannot be captured ... I feel angry with you, angry at you for bringing the truth before me – angry that this is how it is – that you still want me to stay and face my humiliation, the shame of being 'too much'. I cannot understand you, cannot understand how you can bear the frustration it must be for you ... that I seem to be a shape and suddenly the landscape changes and you are dealing with a whole new set of realities.

In supervision, at the time of these letters and sessions as the crisis continued, we had a discussion about the 'duty' mother – the feeling that had been so accurately transferred onto me, of Jane feeling herself to be with a mother who was not loving or attentive but doing her duty. She was re-experiencing with me the deep resentment that she felt towards this mother. I could either talk about and highlight the difference between these mothers or let her use me just like her otherwise preoccupied mother. At this time this was particularly poignant because in my hallway was the baby carriage of my recently born grandchild, although we never explicitly made reference to this. At an unconscious level this highlighted the contrast of her feeling of 'not belonging'.

In this letter she confirms my interpretations and comments:

> I just wanted to go – I felt so humiliated of being where I was not welcomed – with someone who had a responsibility towards me which she finds a burden. This is so familiar – frozen – and I feel humiliated, deeply ashamed at my inability to have anything about me which is engaging.

As we replayed some of the familiar themes in the transference, it occurred to me that when Jane had been like this with her previous therapists – dissociated, frozen and unable to respond, she was replaying the recurring situation with her mother, which she now so clearly describes to me in the transference relationship that we were in. She continued even more graphically with:

> I think this is what I felt – the little girl desperate, desperate to be with you – and you quite unmoved. I think your baby is in the house – means there is no place for a cuckoo in the nest. She is not yours, could never be yours, is long-legged and very blonde and painfully shy – not small dark and energetic and self-confident. She hides in the corner watching you desperate for a crumb ...
>
> I need to get away from you. I can't struggle with you anymore. I need to stay near to you. Can't go ... Can't stay. Can't live. Can't die ... Not alive ... Not dead ... Not well ... Not ill ... Why can't I stop this? Why can't I let you go and stop this?

This ambivalence was to continue through the eight or so weeks leading up to my departure for the end of the year break. Looking back Jane was unconsciously sensing that the work would be drawing to a close, which happened in the following year. She was at this time not aware and neither was I that she was moving towards a place of being able to manage herself and her life without therapy.

The shift in the transference, from the more psychotic and primitive feelings towards me into this more narrative like, neurotic and understandable state, and her own rapidly increasing insight into herself, her own mind, was becoming clearer and clearer.

In the end Jane did not cut back her sessions at this juncture and, on my return, we moved into the final stage of the work. Ending therapy was undoubtedly facilitated by her establishing a relationship with her newly met partner, which was subsequently going to become a loving and mutually supportive and caring marriage. She was clear that her ability to find, make and sustain this intimate and loving relationship with a caring adult had everything to do with how we had negotiated, and she had survived in, our relationship.

In working through her early fear of dependency, pain of closeness and desperate anxiety about abandonment, Jane knew she was now in a position to tolerate the inevitable complexities of being in an intimate relationship with another adult. She could now recognise her archaic relational needs when they arose. She was able to see the difference between realistic needs and unrealistic needs that one adult would have from another adult, rather than the constant seeking to repair the past parental failures in current relationships.

As we came to the end of the last year of regular therapy, Jane had made many changes and was improving session by session. As the drive towards health became stronger than the forces that repeated the past, the ongoing improvement and ever increasing signs of positive development took over. This process was well underway in the final year of the work, while at the same time there seemed to be setbacks or crises yet to be dealt with.

At times the signs of health were often not so easily discernible and Jane still dissociated, still regressed and got very scared, almost up to the end. However, by now in this final phase, she had managed the painful and difficult separation from her husband, moved into a house of her own and was finding a way to live an independent and adult life.

In a session in late November, for example, Jane arrived somewhat grown up, saying that she was moving in the next week and asked if she could call me the day before or the day of the move.

When I readily agreed she was visibly moved. She described to me how she was packing, getting terrified and then recovering; every now and then she looked up and told me how grateful she was as she recognised what had happened in the therapy. She added: 'I keep complaining and you take it'.

Jane also commented that she knew she still needed to go back into the regression. I was moved as I became aware that part of what I witnessed was as if she heard herself as she speaks to me, that she had developed the capacity to take a perspective and see what was happening between us with much more clarity. The session ended with a mutual acknowledgement of the stress and strain of the work and the pain of many years of emotional struggle to reach this point.

By now the transference has shifted profoundly and yet there were still strong transferential aspects to our interaction. As a child it was impossible for Jane to tell her mother anything or trust her with herself in any way. The difference now was that she could bring her experience to me, both her capacity to cope and her fear of still collapsing, as well as her experience of me and her feelings about me. As I remember that her fear was of something which might not be coped with, Jane explained that her fear was of being told off by me. Finding that she is not alone with her anxiety but that I can stand with her, and also hear her criticisms, disappointments and anger about times in the early part of our work, it strengthened her feelings about herself and a trust in her inner reality.

What I spoke about with her, in an important session, was the fear of becoming phobic *as if* there was something that couldn't be faced, *as if* I needed to be protected. What we needed was to find a way through this together and not to treat me as if I was someone who didn't want to know or was unable to hear or bear it.

By the end of this year it was becoming clear that Jane knew and understood the value of this work: that she was able to find herself, with her 'self' given back to her in such a way that she felt restored. She had become able to keep a hold on the good, having come through what had felt like a life and death struggle, without being destroyed or destroying – as others in her family had been.

The road to the end and freedom from the past

It is in Jane's newfound ability to negotiate an intimate adult relationship, which was to lead to a happy and fulfilling outcome, that we see one of the significant gains of the hard work in therapy. I describe this in more detail here because it is the result of the relational capacity that Jane had developed through our therapeutic work together. Shortly after this session, at the end of the year, I left for abroad as usual, and Jane was not in nearly such a state about the break or gap in the work.

During this break we had a number of phone calls while I was away. And it was in this break that Jane met the person who was to become her new partner. That meeting was somehow related to our work but more importantly it was her newly found confidence in herself that cemented the relationship.

At some point during these weeks Jane had called a dating system she discovered on the internet. Then she found someone to talk to – originally, she claimed, out of her feeling of frustration with my inaccessibility. Thus at first the calls were important because she could phone whenever she felt like it, and during the evening or night if she so desired. The main point was that she felt in control, and she had access to this man whenever she felt like it.

During her calls to me Jane still spoke about her anxiety that I would either move back to Africa or Australia, and that she felt she would need me for the rest of her life, emphasising how much she needed to talk to me and how important the calls to me still were to her.

By the time I returned, the new relationship had been established and Jane started her first session somewhat embarrassed and shyly telling me about this man, half expecting me to be disapproving and critical, or possibly jealous and angry with her. They had been on several dates and, as to be expected, she felt like a young teenager 'in love', but worried about it collapsing and being rejected.

In some ways, there were parallels between this relationship and ours. Jane found herself agitating and longing to speak to this man until she heard his voice. They speak every day and she recognised the parallels. She also commented that she feels far more able to cope with a relationship, and with this one, as it became increasingly significant to her. They seemed to be able to have meaningful conversations about their pasts and about themselves, and how it felt to talk to each other: all the signs of intimacy and real relating. She said she could talk to him about things she didn't talk to me about.

Jane talked about her fear of her own capacity to be abusive in close and intimate, potentially dependent, and vulnerable situations.

Her ex-husband carried the violence and capacity for abuse. He was not physically violent towards her but nonetheless she was scared of him, and protective towards her children as she had been with her younger brother in the face of his bullying and emotional attacks.

Since this new relationship began in reaction to the break in therapy, there was some confusion in Jane's mind about it. How does she manage her attraction to him and also her wish to regress and her longing for good parenting? In the beginning her man was still somewhat of a 'dream partner', but fortunately he was able and healthy enough for the external and real nature of who he is, and what their relationship is, to keep confronting her with an external 'other'. This allowed her to manage her inner and outer reality in a more grounded way.[1]

By now the belief in change, growth and a capacity to set limits was apparent as well as how we were now moving rapidly towards completion of a mammoth task. Shortly after my return Jane and her man began to spend the nights together and her anxiety about intimacy was quickly resolved, consolidating the relationship at another level.

The therapy shifted with Jane's growing capacity, and focused on supporting the developing new relationship in the real world, as the groundwork for her worthiness has been laid, and she felt that she deserved to be with someone who treated her well.

Through Jane's release and expression of the rage and craziness in relation to me, she found that they could be managed and contained. She now felt liberated, as she understood her early regressed states and the irrational emotional responses that could be generated belonged to her difficult past and had no place in her current close relationships.

In the final stages of the therapy I found it still essential not to bypass the negative towards me but to create for Jane the experience of being with someone who could stay with the feelings that her mother could not tolerate. She had believed neither she nor any other could tolerate or survive those feelings.

Her primitive feelings were no longer part of Jane's current reality, and they no longer needed to be acted out in a current close relationship, or in seeking a partner who would keep her repeating the past. She had found that she no longer needed a 'better mother' in order to feel safe in the world. And in her life she no longer needed to feel alone as if no-one would be able to be close to her or love her appropriately.

From the therapy Jane learned that she had been unable to set clear boundaries so that, in the past, she would run away rather than attempt to negotiate these in an adult way. In the therapy she had come to appreciate, and felt the value of, being held by clear firm yet flexible boundaries in close relationships.

Soon after my return from my last break Jane commented on the big difference she now experiences. Although she still had some difficulties in her life they are now within the realm of the usual. Her ex-husband was still avoiding completing her financial settlement, but on the other hand things were going really well in the new relationship. And they then travelled together to India where he had a work assignment

Jane mentioned how she was still finding it useful from time to time to keep writing to me, as a way of keeping a check on her inner mind and processing some of her current anxieties. We then made an appointment for three months later, both knowing that we were close to completing an extraordinary journey together.

Some months passed when I received this letter:

> The reason I rang is that I was going to court re the divorce settlement and at the time was highly agitated and felt the need to talk to you. Thanks for your message.
>
> Also I began to wonder about the writing we spoke about – and what I more and more feel would have been helpful to me, and maybe others, is to read – to see someone else's experience in the written word. It helped me to read 'My Kleinian Home' (Nina Herman, 1985) and other accounts of the struggle. I know there have been parallel accounts by patient and therapist of a therapy but somehow this feels different, more raw, more intense, less sanitised and with a different kind of analysis.
>
> What I am suggesting is that we publish a chronological, representative, sample of the letters (identity suitably disguised) together with the matching sessional notes as part of a larger discussion of therapeutic change and theoretical reflection. I think this would have an immediacy and a truth, and therefore more authenticity than anything I could write at this distance ... but could be complemented, on my part, by what I considered was helpful from this distance.

This letter was one of a number of communications expressing the value to her, and her support for, publishing an account of the work. In the end this book goes some way to fulfilling our mutual wish to communicate the essence of a therapy which had become life-changing and enhancing.

Jane then updated me with news that the divorce settlement had gone through in a reasonable way, with compromises on both sides. Now she was feeling free and able to plan a future which included moving closer to her partner and a future date being set for a wedding. She would still travel a few days a week as she moved her practice to the new home. The competent adult mature way in which she described her future plans was largely the result of the hard work we had both done over the years.

She ended this letter as follows:

> I feel well and happy. My kids seem to be doing OK but I don't want to move away just yet. My social life seems far more important than my work life – although I am enjoying that too. So all in all things look very good for me.
>
> I heard your voice and I missed you. It is good to know I could contact you if I need to. I know you are getting ready to fly South for the winter, like lots of other migratory birds. I hope you have a good time – it is good to feel fine even though I know you will be away.
>
> I look forward to reading anything you may write about our work together and possibly collaborating in some small way.
>
> With lots of Love ...

Reflections on the therapy by the patient and the therapist

I will start with some of Jane's reflections some years after the dust had settled. We were no longer meeting in any regular or professional way and I had been thinking about what to write, how to write it and where to start. I was strongly encouraged by my supervisor, who had always felt encouraged by the work and pleased with the outcome, as of course was I. We do like our successes and there seemed to lie in this story much that could be said about the process of long-term, intensive and consistent therapy.

Furthermore, publishing an account of the therapy could show the possibilities of achieving transformational and enduring change that can lead to an enriched capacity for living life. This could provide others with a hope and belief in the value of addressing early childhood trauma, which carries over into life through psychotherapy rather than 'managing' that with psychotropic drugs. I repeat, as she did to me, some of her words here:

> Notwithstanding my current 'sniffiness' about those who work with these methods – I do think something changed which had not been touched in all those years of talking therapy ... to give me what I needed, to get my life back. Maybe in the end we will never find the 'truth' of what helped. It seems to me that it is rather like one of those impromptu meals where you create something by using up all the odds and ends in the fridge and create something superb and wonderful. The more I try to get my mind around what the crucial ingredients were for this successful therapy – the less I seem able to do so.
>
> A few random thoughts [Jane's]:
>
> I wonder about the physiological effects of all those years of holding, reading etc., etc. I remember one of the arguments in support of the re-Childing [a process of inviting the client to regress and behave and be treated as the child they no longer were] was that the brain cannot distinguish between a real and a vividly imagined experience. Although the previous therapist did some of this re-Childing work, it made not a jot of difference.
>
> During my therapy training the cognitive information about early childhood and the long lasting effects of damage and trauma was excruciatingly painful – I sought more and more needing to touch the same place. Long before I came into training I read books like 'I never promised you a rose garden' – about a breakdown – and also Mary Barnes. I knew I would have to breakdown because the structure holding me together was killing me. It was as though I had donned a total plaster cast inside which meant I could never grow strong.
>
> Of course I could never imagine the indescribable hell of the road I would have to travel.
>
> Coming back to the 'parenting' part of our relationship – if the 'holding' didn't do the trick, then what did?
>
> I remember meeting you and hearing you talk – which raised the hope that you would not only hold me but that finally I had met someone who could understand. So it was the combination of feeling understood, your commitment to me, together with your

acceptance of my terrible internal turmoil which made the initial difference. Being able to share that which was experienced as psychotic – perhaps in the end that is what was needed. Certainly that was not enough. I would never have recovered without it.

The letters formed a crucial part of the therapy. To pour out – totally uncensored – that which I had had to contain all my life – ended up saving my life. But as we know, that in and of itself that was not enough. Changing your way of working after first psychological and physical parenting seemed to be equally critical.

The more I think and remember – the less clear I become about which of the elements were the crucial ones. Some of the various workshops in training took me to the edge of breakdown – but somehow I knew enough not to break down fully – to let go until I believed I was in a safe pair of hands.

Once I let go I was lost – there was no going back – so thank God when I became too heavy for your hands you found other hands, i.e. Patrick's, to hold you holding me. Thank you for being committed enough to find what you needed.

My reflections

As I reflect at this stage, many years after the completion of the work which changed both Jane's life and my thinking and understanding of the process – the necessary and sufficient conditions for transformational therapy, the ingredients and factors are multiple and complex.

Much of this book is describing and capturing the process over the course of our work, both from the patient's and from the therapist's points of view. I will conclude with the key issues as I see them and highlight what seems obvious to me.

In the first place the work depended on a patient being deeply committed to change, changing her life and striving for a better way of relating to her children, friends, colleagues and her own clients. Jane understood something about the necessity to fix her relational world, even though consciously the driving force was to free herself from the crippling anxiety, lack of self-confidence, and huge feelings of inadequacy and shame that she suffered from.

I was a motivated therapist, with a good amount of experience behind me by the time we met, yet I knew that there were conditions and therapeutic problems I was unable to solve.

I had experienced getting badly stuck with a client some years before, who had some of the similar issues and yet the course and the process of the therapy was different. I was drawn to Jane, moved by the strength of what seemed to me an almost instantaneous transference, highly idealised and yet compelling. By this time I had experienced forms of this 'idealisation' from clients, patients and students. Although not absolutely clear about my part in co-creating this dynamic, I recognised that there is something crucial about a capacity to pick up, tune in, and to be able to 'hear' the scared, traumatised, often neglected and abused child.

The received wisdom, from my point of view at the time, through the TA training as well as the more general humanistic *'zeitgeist'*, lay in providing a 'corrective emotional experience' – some form of 're-parenting', a better experience for the 'inner child'. For many of my colleagues and friends, our own experience of the regressed cathartic work had seemed to provide both relief and the possibility of finding a new integration in the present, free from earlier distortions and anxieties. I am talking here about the neurotic level of disturbance and related problems.

Applying such logic to those who have had less security in childhood, less internalised integration and coherence, and a more fragmented and fragile sense of 'self', was to prove to be ineffective – at times damaging. It could lead to stuck therapies or some other form of unsatisfactory ending or rupture. I was yet to learn this understanding more clearly.

To return to the major/key factors: we began with a particular fit in terms of motivation, availability, and some of what Jane has described in several places as her belief or hope that she had found what she needed at this stage in her own work.

To say that I underestimated the severity, length and complexity of the work, is no understatement. At the same time I could not foresee the satisfaction, gratification and learning, and extension for me that would result from doing this work.

We both 'hung in', at times against difficult odds. There were moments when the work could have fallen apart, become too difficult and one or other of us could have bowed out. This did not happen however. The various crises are described above. Without doubt, a key factor was finding Patrick Casement as a supervisor. His flexibility and great capacity and experience, and his understanding, carried me intellectually to a place beyond where I had been able to work, and my ability to contain Jane and myself, even though at times I was still puzzled by the meaning of certain processes between us.

One of the major puzzles was how to clearly make sense of and understand the meaning of the psychotic, very primitive, material – primarily accessed by Jane and communicated to me via letters. It was less important to interpret and understand and more necessary to remain open, accepting of what was being expressed, and to treat the material as transferential primitive process: a creative and amazingly effective way of putting emotional rawness into words, to allow it to be contained and captured on paper – in words. It is not a coincidence that what unleashed and triggered this material was initially the art therapy, being conducted in a safe and boundaried place, one that protected me and Jane's relationship to me.

The next factor that cannot be emphasised enough was my understanding, acquired through the supervision, of the importance of the boundaries: thinking about them, holding and managing them, and the realisation that work of this nature rests totally on firm and clear boundaries.

Holding the boundaries, reinforcing them, managing them, then becomes the *fulcrum* to facilitate the 'use of an object' aspect of the work. Another way to describe this is to talk about the centrality of creating the opportunity for the negative transference: to facilitate the process of shifting from an idealised positive transference through a process of disillusionment to the negative.

What remains a question, and is still somewhat unclear to me, is to what extent the early 'better mother' therapy was central to the subsequent therapy. In Jane's mind it was essential, providing her with the trust and the memories of a different experience with me and of me. The long months of soothing, creating a 'corrective emotional experience', providing her with an internal model of being loved, cherished and understood as a child in the therapeutic space, seemed to give her the capacity to tolerate the waves of hatred, rage, violence and terror she felt when she lost sight of me in the current reality; and when she experienced the closeness and intimacy as threatening and dangerous to her very being.

Coinciding with the time of bringing the therapy to an end, Jane was able to meet and establish a good relationship with a suitable partner. She was clear that it was the therapy that had enabled her to find and make this nurturing and life affirming relationship, with its sustainability and deeply nourishing qualities.

In the background to our work together was Jane's training as a counsellor, which provided the intellectual and conceptual basis for her, as well as the previous work and her own ongoing work with others. All these factors contributed to Jane's growing understanding of herself and others, as well as with others.

Finally I feel it necessary to mention her fundamentally sweet, loving nature, intelligence and sensitivity, once liberated from the early damage sustained in her family. That earlier damage had been reinforced in the first marriage. But as she became released from that her loving nature was able to grow and flower when recognised and appreciated: first by her therapist and then by her newfound partner who became her second husband.

For me, working with this patient and the support and learning acquired in the supervision changed my work forever. I was changed both as a therapist, as a supervisor and teacher.

Note

1 I am reminded here of Winnicott's (1971) wonderful notion about how 'play, creativity and the capacity for intimacy occur in a transitional area between our inner and external lives'.

Chapter 8

Some of the theoretical ideas that supported the therapy

This chapter is specifically addressed to therapists, supervisors and counsellors, although it may also be of interest to coaches, mentors and consultants or others interested in the theory of the work. I will only elaborate on the central ideas which arise from this work and are well illustrated by the clinical material.

I will add how this piece of therapy became instrumental to me in clarifying an overall theoretical position which subsequently described my view of the work. Other theoretical notions have been well described by others in various places (see reference list) so I will only refer to them without elaborating well-understood clinical ideas.

A comment on the place of theory in clinical work

Theory in psychotherapy has mostly been developed from clinical cases. One could think of this process as analogous to the 'case law' development in the legal field. The clinical case described here is particularly interesting from a theoretical perspective. Much of the underlying approach rests on psychodynamic developmental theory, which postulates the significance of early life to subsequent adult functioning.

The central idea is that early organising principles shape our inner and relational world, and that trauma and deprivation in childhood are significant factors in causing later problems in life, and particularly in our relational worlds. This fundamental argument lays the basis for an approach to therapy, which rests on the relationship that therapist and patient form. The quality, intensity and the co-created nature, but also the evolving and developmental aspects of the therapeutic relationship, are crucial.

Thus the relational field forms the arena in which the therapy occurs, and the description of this relationship follows the trajectory of the work. The how, the what and the why lie in an understanding of the relationship between the participants in the work. Therefore this is essentially a story of a relationship. How it was formed, how it developed, the changing nature and the number of levels or dimensions that it contained.

Theoretical orientations to the work serve a number of functions. The frame guides the therapist as well as providing a container for the anxiety and uncertainty that therapy generates. I have come to understand that clinical work is supported by a theory of human nature and functioning, and by clinical methods or techniques.

In the first place there is the general view or understanding of human nature. The clinical work described here is very clearly located in a frame that would be described as a form of Relational and Integrative Psychotherapy. At the time of doing the work I was not so clearly calling my approach a Relational one. I had read, and been influenced by, Stephen Mitchell (1988) and his colleagues, who were describing themselves as Relational Psychoanalysts. The Relational Transactional Analysts were to form later.

In terms of methodology, a Relational approach sees itself as focusing on the interaction between therapist and client/patient, rather than the pole of the patient's self or that of the other. Although this was not how I had initially framed the work, the supervision with Patrick Casement kept the interaction between us as the main focus of the work.

Writing this book has similarities to the therapy, in that one of my dilemmas has been how best to use the patient's words, which were captured so exquisitely in the letters, and then how to tie these to my understanding, my supervision and sessional notes. The work with ordering, sequencing and being challenged with how best to pull all my material into a coherent and logical order felt like a co-created process. This document itself carries multiple sources and voices. It is a description from the perspective of a two-person psychology and further a Relational Psychology: one in which my subjectivity as therapist and author is embedded throughout.

I was teaching Integrative Psychotherapy on several training programmes and courses in the UK, and talking at conferences and workshops as an Integrative Psychotherapist. In my mind, what I was describing was a perspective from Developmental Psychology, based on psychoanalytical ideas of early development and its significance to later personality structure and function, from a humanistic philosophical point of view. This description still, to a degree, covers my current views. The contemporary evidence from neuroscience and research on the efficacy of psychotherapy, confirming the centrality of the relationship to the outcome of psychotherapy, are also important factors that guide the work, as do some of the concepts derived from Bowlby's Attachment Theory (Bowlby, 1973, 1980, 1982).

In addition to an overall approach from which to conceptualise the work, there is also a theory of methods or technique. I want to describe the most significant ones, as herein lies the clarity that I acquired over the course of this work and the impact of the supervision. It was this growing understanding, I believe, that supported me to do the work in the way that I did and bring it to a satisfactory conclusion.

By the time I undertook this work I was an experienced therapist, nonetheless there were certain things that were not clear to me, in particular managing and working through intense negative and at times psychotic transferential experiences. Through the supervision I acquired a clarity about these concepts which form a significant base for therapy, in particular, working long-term with the negative transference and the countertransference problems that are evoked. In extreme circumstances, failure to contain and manage some of these transferences results in serious ruptures, impasses, and breakdowns in the work, with the potential for 'acting out' and sometimes serious problems – for example stalking.

The use of an object

This is one of those profound concepts that help and contain the rocky road of the necessary negative transference, supporting therapists through the experience of the attacks that occur during the work. It is a unique and powerful opportunity for the patient/client to have a different experience in relation to their emotional distress, rage, frustration and deep grief. As Winnicott (1971) indicates, it is an idea that arises from his view of the earliest stages of life, occurring in the baby's experience of the world. In an omnipotent state of mind, in which infants believe they are the centre of their universe, when they are angry, rageful and frustrated and they are left alone with these feelings, they can feel as if they have destroyed the object. Also they have not yet understood that the object (mother) has (her) own mind and locus of control.

When the baby's experience becomes such that the object survives their real and imagined attacks, and is not destroyed by their phantasised attacks or rage, they can gradually develop the understanding that the object (mother) is separate from them: she has her own mind and survives by her own ability. Paraphrasing Winnicott, the baby's experience is something like: 'Hello Object ... I've destroyed you ... but thanks for surviving ... because now I can use you, knowing that you are outside my omnipotent control.' Explaining the process like this helps to concretise something that actually originates in very early experience, nonverbal or preverbal, unremembered and unconscious.

Although this is a critical developmental step or stage, in the task of distinguishing inner from outer worlds, and developing a separate sense of self, many adults haven't adequately completed this stage of early development. The parent needs to manage their infant's distress well enough, and particularly extreme states of emotion. It is necessary to survive being killed off in the mind of the raging child. The beauty of this clinical material is how graphically, explicitly and directly the patient puts this into words: 'her wishes and desires both to murder me and also torture and torment me'.

Clinically I would translate these ideas into meaning that we need to survive, as therapists, *whatever we become in the mind of the patient*. We need to become able to tolerate becoming the 'bad object', often the monsters and monstrous representations from childhood that have been part of the child's experience, and their treatment by the adults, who were charged with their care and meeting their needs. The survival of the therapy by both participants involves not retreating or attacking back, and also not deflecting the client through too forceful transference interpretations to protect 'the self' of the therapist.

There was a time when Patrick asked whether in fact she could become too much, as the barrage and flood of letters persisted with their vicious and multiple ways to make mad attacks on me. This fragment of a letter captures something from a session, well into this phase of the work, where Jane already has a good deal of insight into her process and is on the road to using me as a representation of her inner monsters.

> I realise that the censor is allowing a little more room to move, a little more to be seen. He must trust you to do the 'holding'.

I can get overwhelmed and frightened – but I did feel you as very solid – and solidly with me. I was surprised at what got through today. The little girl is cross again.

We can make the assumption that Jane had got through the developmental challenge that is described as the ability to 'use the object', as a representation of the good and bad mother – evidenced by the amount of splitting, projection and delusion that she showed in her transference to me.

I will now focus on the point in the work when the disturbing and psychotic-like letters reached a crescendo. The letters were arriving sometimes several in a day and all contained violence, attacks and phantasies of perpetrating a lot of physical and painful harm on me. They were intensely physical and concrete. In fact Jane complained a good deal of feeling a lot of pain, pins and needles, cramps, catching her breath. She had certainly somatised her psychic pain strongly.

While I was being seen as the 'good object', Jane believed, unconsciously, that *she* had created me and was forcing me to remain the good object for her. Some of her massive anxiety in relation to me was that either she or the 'good object' could be destroyed by her hatred and rage.

The survival of these attacks, on the part of the therapist, disturbs the patient's magical thinking. It allows the patient to come to a new, different and more realistic relationship to the external world of others, with whom they are relating.

At this time too, Jane had the delusion that she could get back and replay the 'happy childhood' she felt so desperately deprived of, that with me in the role of the 'pretend good mother', and her in the role of the loving sweet child, we were going to re-write history. Persisting with these views, Jane kept feeling that she didn't know how she was going to get better without bringing the 'little girl' to me. Her image of being re-parented by a 'better' mother, and her idea that the therapy would come about in this way, was deeply embedded in her mind.

Jane linked the 'mad stuff' she began to experience as being engendered by the deprivation she felt from me, through my withdrawal from the role of 'better mother'. My response to her was that the frustration provoking the anger needed necessarily to be brought to me. In making this intervention I refrained from making any transference comments.

What had happened as a result of the shift I made, both physically and metaphorically, was that I had become very close to the 'bad object' in her mind. The phantasy now became that I was deliberately replicating her mother's cruelty, with the capacity to hurt her in a variety of ways, some of which can only be guessed at. This shows how the past is activated in the present relationship. At the same time, Jane had also at times experienced me as the mother who is cool and distant.

She said:

> I have read plenty of the books – I know the importance of the negative transference – but what feels wrong are the lengths to which you would go to replicate my mother's treatment of me.
>
> I'll go mad and kill myself and then you will be sorry. It will be all your fault ... I'll murder and slash and blame you for not holding me ... I feel so crazy as I write this – a battle field, lots of activity going on inside ... I need someone to help me to soothe, to bear all this activity ... pins and needles in my head.

The therapeutic response, which Patrick had helped me formulate in supervision, to these ongoing pleas both in the letters and also in the sessions, sounded something like: 'You find it very difficult to imagine that anyone could really be in touch with you when you feel so uncontained. Thus I can now know directly how you feel when you feel uncontained and more significantly when you feel left by me.'

That many of these attacks were confined initially to the letters helped me to remain non-retaliatory, and reflective, and gave me the time and space to process them and feed back to her in manageable doses. The person in Jane's mind would not have been able to do this, and certainly would not have welcomed her sharing her feelings about how she believed she was being treated by them. There is an intense and overpowering wish to punish the mother who wasn't there for her, and who was unable to be in touch with her child.

This material graphically and explicitly puts into words Jane's desire to murder me, and torture and torment me, to get me to know how much pain she was feeling. The images were terrifying to her as well as to me as they were so concrete and explicit.

As the therapist, I was able to hold onto knowing that my task included being able to tolerate becoming the 'bad object', the monster and the monstrous representations from childhood, and to tolerate the child's anguish at the neglect and the verbal abuse. At some point my supervisor was becoming concerned that she might really become too much for me, by the level, intensity and frequency of the letters and the material contained in them.

I had always experienced Jane's writing as a singularly creative means to express some of her internal experience, particularly when I became the target as central to evoking and unleashing it. However I was protected by the material being in writing rather than being more directly in the room. Even with the distance created by the letters, I was not without worry and concern about how she seemed at times to be unravelling. A helpful factor was that, by this stage in the work, I was getting feedback from outside our work about how Jane was beginning to show marked and dramatic improvements in her real world. This was before any improvement was evident in the sessions or letters.

Jane's ambivalence and growing capacity was expressed in a letter at the time when the changes were beginning in the third to fourth year:

> ... staying and being reasonable: I want to say 'it's not fair', 'I hate you', I don't want you for my Mummy. All that and you stay, don't get afraid. Don't persecute, bully, shame, or reject. Don't want much do I?

The 'good mother' is there for the 'bad'. So part of what she was expressing was a wish to punish me for being willing and able to receive her feelings. If no-one is willing to hear her it justifies her parents' failure. She is now continually coming closer to the point of that recognition at this stage in the work.

As I withstood the pressure, helped by the fact that the worst and a lot of it was initially contained in letters, gradually Jane became more able to say these things directly in sessions and thus no longer needed to communicate them in letters.

If there is a conclusion to be drawn from this it is that a genuinely good experience in therapy is in finding that the other can be there for the bad and frightening feelings, without a need to be defensive or to retaliate for the perceived and experienced attacks. Through reading the letters with the lens of the 'use of an object' it becomes possible to remain in touch emotionally with the patient, and retain one's own mind and capacity to think.

Containment

In many ways this idea is central to all forms of effective psychotherapy. Paying attention to the various forms of boundaries requires constant vigilance. From the beginning with Jane, boundary maintenance was a challenge for both of us. Intuitively she had understood that she needed to protect and safeguard her therapy space with me. As she lived in another city, she travelled throughout the therapy – separating and keeping a clear boundary around her therapy, for herself, as far as possible.

Some of the greatest crises in the work were in fact generated by contact or processes outside of the boundaries. As the work progressed, however we both understood how central it was for us to be alert to those situations, where the real world could leak into our therapeutic space and relationship.

As I understood more specifically how the boundaries, the holding of them and the clarity around them, impacted on the work, I was able to constantly think about them. I now believe that, in order to effectively allow/create the optimal conditions for the 'use of an object' boundary, management is critical.

A further issue that arises when considering the boundaries, has to do with the letters. Letters, phone calls and other forms of extra sessional contact are all boundary issues. Initially, the letter writing had started as a way of maintaining contact, and providing some sort of holding or bridging during the breaks and gaps in the work. From a relational perspective, keeping in touch in this way during long breaks in the work has some legitimacy. But once the letters began escalating, at times becoming a bombardment in between sessions, it raised the question of how to think about and manage these communications between us. Jane recognised herself that there was an issue here and on more than one occasion expressed her gratitude that I allowed the letters.

As I worked with how to think about and deal with the letters, and discussed this question in supervision, it seemed to me that the letters were a valuable and unique form of communication between us. Blocking them would prevent me from having access to what was going on, and could prevent Jane from finding what her own experience was.

I was grateful that the obsessive and compulsive nature of how Jane started to write, and the fact that she was using writing rather than far more destructive processes, was a relief to me in terms of the anxiety that could have been generated and communicated in other ways. Over and above all these practical considerations, the fact that there was now another medium, a 'post sessional' forum for communication, unquestionably accelerated, aided and supported the work, as it provided a rich source of insight and understanding of the patient's inner world.

We never read the letters together in a session and I would only refer to them lightly but in such a way as to show that I had read and thought about them. As the work finished I discussed with Jane the fact that I had all her letters, sequenced in order of the dates written, and I asked her if she wanted them back. But, in a sense, giving the letters back could have been seen as returning to her, her old undigested material. Not surprisingly she was clear that she had no interest in getting them back. She said in fact: 'the letters are yours to do with what you want'.

I knew what a unique and valuable documentation of inner distress and the therapeutic process these letters were, but only in completing this manuscript does their contribution become really clear. One of the challenges was how to extract, from hundreds of pages of letters, enough of the content. In this script there are extracts and fragments which I feel give a sufficient feel and flavour of Jane's internal experience to highlight the value of 'allowing', or rather receiving and being able to use and pay serious attention to, the letters.

Some of what Jane had been able to paint, write about and finally tell me, falls into what Winnicott described as 'unendurable agonies' of the infant, and the adult patient, when the pain of unmet needs seems unbearable. The notion of these experiences is that they are indescribable, and yet that in itself is a way to put into words, or finding another way to symbolise, the quality of the feelings.

Jane's internal state could have been described as 'on the edge' of a breakdown or in 'fear of a breakdown'. That she found the capacity to carry on appearing to function in a somewhat normal way was due to her capacity to dissociate from the current reality. As the dissociations began to break down, Jane often experienced herself closer to the breakdown she was working so hard to protect herself from.

Holding and containing

A book published by one of the American Relational Psychoanalysts, Joyce Slochower, prompts us to think more about the unanswered questions from another perspective. Slochower's view is that certain patients require a long period of 'holding' in the treatment. During this time the analyst protects the patient from directly needing to deal with the analyst's own subjectivity, by not making interpretations or confrontations.

Although this does not describe exactly how I had been working earlier on in the work, Slochower (1996) makes the point that 'Within the maternal metaphor not only is the patient a baby in crucial ways, but the analyst becomes, at least in part, the maternal object. As a maternal object, the analyst's behaviour and affective responses mirror those of her patient. Even more importantly, the analyst's symbolic function overrides her interpretative one and in some cases is essential to cure' (p. 15).

The above view seems consistent enough with the present case to provide some confirmation that, for a certain period of time in therapy, creating a safe unquestioned state of feeling held by the therapist is powerful, and perhaps necessary, in creating the base from which to withstand the vicissitudes of the negative and often persecutory feelings that will occur during a phase of the 'use of an object'. One could in fact go further and see that both the positive phase of idealisation and then the necessary disillusionment together form Winnicott's notion of the use of the object, as the infant understands that both experiences are of the same mother and the extreme nature of both positive and negative belong together.

A note on dissociation as a defence

'We believe that dissociation is the key concept to understanding traumatization', thus Van der Hart, Nijenhuis and Steele (2006) open their important contribution describing structural dissociation as the central response to chronic and usually early trauma. Jane's difficulties could be understood from this point of view. The various internal states that she was in touch with, and the fact that there was an external presentation that could be described as an 'Apparently Normal Personality' (APN), fits well into their conceptualisation as the adult manifestation of chronic and debilitating trauma in childhood.

In various forms, Jane was aware of such split off parts in herself as 'the grey baby', the 'devil child' and most centrally 'the little girl'. These parts are all forms of what the authors of *The Haunted Self* call 'Emotional Parts' (EPs).

Van der Hart et al. (2006) follow Janet's seminal work and see the split off parts, and their separation from each other, as a way in which the personality manages overwhelming anxiety and how it deals with the ongoing shocks that trauma creates for the self. The authors argue that the lack of cohesion and integration of the personality is a consequence of how there is a constant re-experiencing of trauma on the one hand, and an attempt to avoid reminders or memories of trauma on the other.

Although published long after the completion of the work, this therapy followed the model of addressing the splitting, and creating space and the possibility for the integration of the repressed and split off parts.

As it became increasingly obvious that the therapy was reaching a satisfactory ending, the various parts seemed to disappear or become integrated in the personality. Most importantly they were being translated into memory, rather than needing to be embodied and re-enacted in the regressed and dissociated states that she so often presented to me in the therapy.

On making mistakes

In this work I made a number of mistakes such as the residential conference, underestimating the effect of the art therapy, and others mentioned as I told the story. Whether and where they helped or hindered the process remains to be understood.

Jane speaks of the tolerance that many patients have when their therapists get things wrong and says:

> What was interesting was that, even though I held you in a kind of enormous positive transference, I didn't need you to be perfect. I didn't need you to get it right all the time. It's odd really. It's not the kind of idealisation where you are the perfect person, where you never get things wrong. It was much more, I think, about commitment. I felt you were committed to me and to our work. So, even when we got into a messy state or things were wrong, somehow your commitment was there. I think that was the important thing, not that you never made a mistake or always understood things perfectly.

Shortly after I started the psychoanalytic supervision, as an attempt to elicit some negative feelings, I remember saying to Jane something like: 'You must be very disappointed. When we started working I had such a reputation and you had high hopes of things changing quickly, whereas it's taking so long and you are still feeling bad a lot of the time.' As I said before, her response was a wonderful example of the unconscious communication between us, in that she said:

> One thing I know about you is that if you don't know something you will make an effort to find out.

This seemed like a direct but unconscious communication about her awareness that I was engaged in a new learning process.

The issue of commitment raised here is also important. In my view, patients and clients who really get well, those who change and transform their lives and themselves, are those who make an absolute commitment to therapy. They display a 'whatever it takes' factor. When I said this to Jane, she commented on the reciprocal commitment that the therapist makes to the patient, to the work and to the process. Here too we have her words, just quoted, about her sense of my commitment and what it meant to her.

Thus the therapy moved into a new phase and her distress was palpable. While things got much more difficult and painful between us, I also breathed a sigh of relief because I could now feel that we were getting unstuck. There was still a long way to go and we were clearly not out of the woods. And I did not have any idea then of how long the process would take, but I began to feel that a necessary change in the work was happening and something new was going to be possible for her and between us.

All this time I was experiencing the important support of my supervisor, and that made all the difference in navigating these then uncharted waters.

Jane's reflection about the changed therapeutic approach that had begun to create both a new, real and powerfully different, dynamic between us was:

> I don't think so. I think that what was right was that alone[1] would not have done the trick. I could not have tolerated the pain. Either I would simply not have contacted that aspect of myself, like I had not in any other therapy previously. I had a way of managing to stay intact and working in a sensible way.

We had been looking at things in a way that essentially left me untouched. It would have helped me to cope better but I would still have been untouched. It was the experience of the regression that caused me to break down. I mean, looking back, I had a major breakdown. I kept walking and working while the breakdown lasted several years.

The unanswered question: the note on which to end

In completing this chapter on some of the central theoretical questions, I come back to what I would consider to be the unanswered question that this work has raised. The question remains for me and for the patient, one that perhaps has no clear answer. After my experience of this work, and the way in which the theory of the 'use of an object' provided the support for managing the negative transference, the importance of facilitating this opportunity for patients and clients became firmly rooted in my own approach to thinking and working clinically.

The question that Jane raised for me, which remains unanswered, was whether it would have been possible for her to remain engaged in the work at that crucial time if she had not first had the long period of holding and positive experience, a form of the 'corrective emotional experience'. The long time in which Jane felt herself to be the little girl gave her the experience and memory of being with me in another emotional relationship. Throughout the time when she was both terrified and enraged with me, she also had another experience of me being caring, kind and gentle, and her being acceptable and valued. During the attacks on me, Jane kept finding my response to be different to her feared phantasy of what it might be, as well as different to what her mother's would have been.

Her belief was that the long period of good experience had laid the foundation of trust, and had created the platform for us to sustain the attacks that were to ensue. She is now convinced that she would have been unable to tolerate the feelings that were aroused in her in relation to me without her previous experience with me.

I don't know whether this is so or not. I do know that often patients leave therapy without an explanation to the therapist, when something of this nature may be going on. We had certainly had times which came close to a rupture which could have ended the therapy prematurely.

Integrative Relational Therapy: towards a psychology of relationship

My view of the work is one that rests on the therapist's use of themselves, which is so clearly illustrated here. It is that the work is: 'All about you and nothing to do with you at the same time'. In this sense, I see this piece of work as being a primary example of relational therapy, and the psychology underlying work of this nature is a Relational Psychology or a Psychology of Relationship. The therapist's self, their sense of themselves and the idea of 'who they are', is as much at risk as that of the patient. It is therefore about a relational psychology and is firmly located in what is known in contemporary theories of psychotherapy as a two-person psychology

This leads to what I have called working with 'You and I'. What I mean by this is that much of the conversation in the session is about the relationship between therapist and patient. In other words there is a lot of exchange, often initiated by the therapist, of the experience of each and their responses to the other. In this sense the therapist's self-disclosure to the patient of the therapist's immediate experience, thoughts and feelings, creates a unique experience of being with someone who opens a window to them, of what are his or her thoughts and feelings about their relationship. This dialogue allows for the real and transferential relationship, both, to be continually at the forefront of the therapy.

From this point of view, implicit in what I am saying is that the stance taken to the transferential and projected aspects of the patient's experience of the therapist is to treat it *as if* it is real, knowing that there is always an element of truth in the projections. While at the same time we need to hold the transferential elements, and thus work in the space I have described as 'about me' and also 'not about me' at the same time.

This can be regarded as a summing up of my view of the work in which I talk about 'Using the Self in psychotherapy' and 'understanding the self' from a Relational Psychology perspective. I believe that all the evidence points to a growing understanding in the field that we are in an era of developing a Relational Psychology as the broad frame, within which to conceptualise work that rests on the practitioner's use of themselves as their central tool in the work.

Note

1 In other words my creating the conditions for her to find me as the better mother rather than the failing 'better mother'.

Afterword

Andrew Samuels

You often hear that it is risky to be too quick to translate the input from a new supervision into clinical action. Surely this will only confuse the patient? And both Shmukler and Casement are indeed careful to reassure their more cautious readers that they took their time. But, to this reader at least, their assessment that the patient was absolutely ready for a shift in perspective accurately captured the facts on the ground, and all three people involved just got on with it pretty damn quickly. I am glad that they did because it shows the rest of us that if it is broke it should be fixed. One can be too reflective and cautious and then the question arises: for whose benefit is this reflection and caution really being done? Maybe one has to trust the patient – as many humanistic pioneers of psychotherapy taught, rather at odds with Freud.

Jane, the patient, as she so often did, expressed the risks in the matter succinctly and forcefully: 'I am scared others will counsel you out of honouring my complexity ... I'm scared of the change in you, the change in your style – scared that you will retreat behind an analytic mask and I will lose you forever'.

Jane was also a psychotherapist and perhaps she had, as so many have over the years, projected onto the contemporary relational analyst many of the worst features of the classic psychoanalytic game: silent, continent, reserved, rigid and so on. But what Shmukler knew from her work with Casement, who surely modelled it for her during their supervision, was that one can be warm and related – and also boundaried, reflective and kind.

When Shmukler writes about Casement's input, she most often uses words like 'help' and 'support'. I think this misses what is surely apparent to any reader – Casement's involvement was not just as helper or supporter but was red-hot and passionate, maybe as the father of the patient to Shmukler's mother (and maybe sometimes it was the other way round). They became a couple of a certain sort and, whilst the use of the word 'erotic' will embarrass both of them (though it shouldn't), there was a sense of an eros connection and relatedness between them as he held her holding the patient as the entire set-up became transmogrified via the supervisory process.

The erotics of supervision – in this wider sense – is an area not as yet much theorised. How I see it working in this case is that the preoccupation of supervisor and psychotherapist with their work created the ground or conditions for the clinical work itself. And the work was Jane.

The learning for me is that we may want to think about dropping our official consensus – honoured in the breach as much as in the observance – that the supervisor stay removed from the case, remembering that *it is not his case* and believing his job to be Zeus-like – surveying things from on high. There is no evidence that this smug fantasy works as a basis for supervision.

Getting a bit more specific, and with my Jungian hat on, I can see that Casement communicated to Shmukler that regression is not only a literal matter, as in regression to infancy. It is also a matter of perspective and the way in which experience is digested. So it was not a matter of a regression in a concrete sense that was needed but a regression to a whole way of functioning psychologically that adults are supposed to do without – but which stubbornly returns as we play, make art, and enjoy the purposelessness (sic) of life.

I think most therapists have had patients that want us to fail for a whole host of reasons, and Jane was deeply committed in the early stages to causing Shmukler to fail. You could call this a piece of primary masochism. Or you could say she was hoping that her attempt to create a failed mother would itself fail. But, to my mind, it was Casement's shrewd realisation that the patient was not in fact desiring what it seemed so apparently obvious she desired that did the trick. Managing her disappointment that the wounds were unhealable was Jane's royal road to healing, not overcoming or mastering them. So I would follow Rumi here: 'Failure is the key to the kingdom'.

The last clinical point I want to raise in this Afterword concerns the role played by 'cleanliness' in this case. How this worked was somewhat counter-intuitive. I saw Shmukler's pre-Casement working in the good mother area as pretty clean. Casement's perspective, apparently more clear and crystalline, was, in truth, much dirtier.

When I was asked to have a look at the book with a view to contributing, I did have a political concern that Casement would be positioned as the psychoanalytic rescuer of a humanistic and integrative practitioner who had somewhat lost her way. Psychoanalysis would be like the Europeans in Apartheid South Africa, humanistic and integrative psychotherapy like the African population. I was relieved to find that this kind of triumphalistic 'schoolism' is not present in the book.

Bibliography

Bowlby, J. (1973) *Attachment and Loss, Vol. 2. Separation: Anxiety and Anger.* New York: Basic Books.
Bowlby, J. (1980) *Attachment and Loss, Vol. 3. Loss, Sadness and Depression.* New York: Basic Books.
Bowlby, J. (1982) *Attachment and Loss, Vol. 1. Attachment.* London: Hogarth Press, originally published 1969.
Casement, P. (1985) *On Learning from the Patient.* London and New York: Tavistock Publications.
Casement, P. (1990) *Further Learning from the Patient: The Analytic Space and Process.* London: Routledge.
Casement, P. (2002) *Learning from our Mistakes: Beyond Dogma in Psychoanalysis and Psychotherapy.* Hove, UK: Brunner-Routledge.
Davis, M. and Wallbridge, D. (1981) *Boundary and Space: An Introduction to the Work of D.W. Winnicott.* London: Karnac.
Fowlie, Heather and Charlotte Sills (eds) (2011) *Relational Transactional Analysis: Principles in Practice.* London: Karnac.
Greenberg, J.R. and Mitchell, S.A. (1983) *Object Relations in Psychoanalytic Theory.* Cambridge, Mass. and London: Harvard University Press.
Hargaden, H. and Sills, C. (2002) *Transactional Analysis: A Relational Perspective. Advancing Theory in Therapy.* Hove, UK: Brunner-Routledge.
Herman, N. (1985) *My Kleinian Home.* London: Quartet Books.
Likierman, M. (2001) *Melanie Klein: Her Work in Context.* London: Continuum.
Mitchell, S.A. (1988) *Relational Concepts in Psychoanalysis: An Integration.* Cambridge, Mass. and London: Harvard University Press.
Mitchell, S.A. and Aron, L. (1999) *Relational Psychoanalysis: the Emergence of a Tradition.* Hillsdale, NJ: Analytic Press.
Pine, P. (1985) *Developmental Theory and Clinical Process.* New Haven: Yale University Press.
Segal, H. (1981) *Melanie Klein.* Middlesex, England: Penguin Books.

Shmukler, D. (2011) 'The use of the self in psychotherapy', in *Relational Transactional Analysis*, edited by Heather Fowlie and Charlotte Sills. London: Karnac.

Slochower, J.A. (1996) *Holding and Psychoanalysis: A Relational Perspective*. New York: The Analytic Press.

Van der Hart, O., Nijenhuis, E.R.S. and Steele, K. (2006) *The Haunted Self: Structural Dissociation and the Treatment of Chronic Traumatization*. New York and London: W.W. Norton and Company.

Winnicott, D.W. (1971) *Playing and Reality*. London: Tavistock. Reprinted Pelican Books, 1974. Penguin Books 1980.

Winnicott, D.W. (1974) 'Fear of Breakdown.' *International Review of Psychoanalysis*. I:103–107.

Winnicott, D.W. (1982a) *Through Paediatrics to Psychoanalysis*. London: Hogarth Press. (first published 1958).

Winnicott, D.W. (1982b) *The Maturational Processes and the Facilitating Environment: Studies in the Theory of Emotional Development*. London: Hogarth Press (first published 1965).

Wright, K. (1991) *Vision and Separation: Between Mother and Baby*. North Vale, NJ: J. Aronson.

Index

abandonment 88
abuse 53–4
acting out 72, 91, 121
affect: high levels of 32; working with 9
aggression 12, 35, 81; hidden 5–6; towards therapist 27
agony, unendurable 77–8, 81, 127
anger, escalation of 57
Apparently Normal Personality (APN) 128
Aron, Lewis 73
art therapist 23–5, 45, 47–8, 55–6, 73–4
art therapy 22–6, 36, 45–57; impact of 45–56; and psychosis 24–5, 86
attachment 71
Attachment Theory 121

baby: grey 49, 58, 87, 128; removal of 81
Barnes, Mary 113
behaviourism 30
boundaries 53, 116, 126; recovery of 73–4
Bowlby, John 121
breakdown 1; on edge of 127
Bruner, Jerome 31

case study *see* Jane
Casement, Patrick 19–22, 27, 34, 36, 57, 69–75, 87, 91, 114–15, 120, 122, 124, 133–5
catharsis 6
change: commitment to 114; irrevocable path to 77–82; seen through letters 91–2
child: destructive 122; 'Devil's' 90, 103, 128; hearing the 115; inner 33, 42, 115; needy 77; patient role as 9

Child Ego State 33, 42
childhood, recovery of 38
chronology, of therapy 34–6
cleanliness 54, 134
clinical work, place of theory in 119–21
commitment 130
communication, written 15
conflict, in therapy 62–3
connection 88
containment 126–7; and holding 127–8
control, manipulated by seating 75
corrective emotional experience 131
countertransference 71, 121
crisis: and boundaries 126; precipitation of 26–7, 77
cruelty: in childhood 11; images of 60
cupboard love 98

defence, dissociation as a 128–9
dependency 43; absolute 87; fear of 107
depression 7
destructiveness 89
development, moments and background in 42
Developmental Psychology 8, 120
disgust 76
dissociation 61, 65, 87; as a defence 128–9
dissociative personality disorder 11
drug abuse 11

early development 33
Ego 83; frozen 38–9, 41
emotion: and language 43; and metaphor 43
Emotional Parts (EPs) 128

enactment, creation of 27
envy 14
Erikson, Erik 31
experience, emotionally corrective 10

fear, of phobia 108
feelings, expression of 9
freedom, from the past 108–12

Gestalt therapy 8, 32, 72, 82
girl: cross 57–9; little 37–43, 46, 58, 64, 66, 68, 70, 83–4, 128; traumatised 63
Greenberg, Jay 73
group therapy 33
group work, crises in 7

hatred, early 98
healing connection, letters as 90–1
Herman, Nina 111
holding, and containing 127–8
hope, importance of 28
humanism 82, 115
humiliation 19, 25

idealisation 57–68, 115
identification, by group 6
images, of cruelty 60
initial meeting 3–4
insanity, and sanity 17–18
Integrative Approach 22, 91
Integrative Psychotherapy 120
Integrative Relational Therapy 132

Jane: agitation and anxiety of 61; chronology of therapy 3–30, 34–6; confusion of 81–2; dissociated states of 87–8; family background of 10–11; marriage breakdown 104, 111–12; needs of 74–5; post-sessional processing by 85–6; psychotic material 116; rage and terror of 59, 110; reflections on therapy by 112–14; relationships of 103–4, 109–11, 116; role as child 9; second marriage of 107, 111; self-censorship by 17, 84–5, 98; sense of self 73, 103–4; story of 1–3; as a therapist herself 7, 117, 133; thoughts on publication 2–3,

111–12; use of letters by 84–5, 91–2, 114; violence of 28–9; words of 1–2
Jungian analysis 19–20

Klein, Melanie 98

language, and emotion 43
letters 36, 114, 125; attacking phantasies in 67; boundary issues with 126; change seen through 91–2; complexity of 58; contribution to therapy 14–18, 83–102; as 'healing connection' 90–1; multiple uses of 100–2; reflecting change in approach and therapy 87–90; as a relationship 101–2; self-soothing aspect of 94–6; violent/psychotic 53, 123–4

madness 49–50, 52, 81, 89; and sanity 96–9
marriage 35
memories, capturing of 92–4
metaphor, and emotion 43
mistakes 129–31
Mitchell, Stephen 73, 120
mood, shifts in 65
mother 11; bad 10, 124–5; better 37–43, 70, 116; failing 35, 57–68; idealised 58; as object 121–2; withholding cold 62, 64–5, 124

neglect, in childhood 11
Nijenhuis, Ellert 128
notes *see* session notes

object: good vs. bad 67; use of 33, 66–7, 97, 101, 116, 121–5, 131
Object Permanence 95
Object Relations 8

paintings *see* art therapy
paranoia 11
parent, therapist role as 9
Parent Interviews 10
past, freedom from 108–12
patient: tolerance of 129, *see also* Jane
phantasies, attacking 67
phobia, fear of 108
phone calls: boundary issues with 126; problems with 18–19; sessions by 87

Piaget, Jean 31
possessiveness 14
presenting issues 6
psychology, of relationship 132
psychosis 97–8, 116; and art therapy 24–5, 52, 86
psychotherapy: theory in 119–21; using yourself in 132

rage, feelings of 89, 116
re-Childing 113
re-decisional approach 34
re-parenting 9, 13–15, 21–2, 103; idealised mother style of 58; model 37–43
recovery 1
regression 21, 134; as defence 77; depth of 9; internal 76, 83; negotiated 8; perpetual 70; return to 108; to little girl state 38–43; training in 32
rejection 62
Relational and Integrative Psychotherapy 120
Relational Psychoanalysts 73, 120
Relational Transactional Analysis 73, 120
relationship: letters as 101–2; psychology of 132
reparative experience 71
residential conference 13–14
resolution 29–30
revulsion 76, 100
role playing 9–10, 41, 72, 91
Rumi, Jalal al-Din 134

sanity: and insanity 17–18; and madness 96–9
saviour, therapist as 5
Self Psychology 8
self-censorship 17, 84–5, 98
self-harm 16, 60–1
self-soothing, quality of 94–6
session notes: 25 April 75–7; in fourth year 53–4, 63–5, 105; from therapy 21, 50–1
Shmukler, Diana 133–4; career of 30–4
siblings: aggression towards 81; relationships with 10–11
Slochower, Joyce 127–8

South Africa 31–2
Steele, Kathy 128
suicide 24, 105
supervision 69, 112, 115–16; and changing work view 73–5; erotics of 134; impact of 70–3; internal 71; notes 54–6, 80; of therapy 20–2, 27, 36, 66–7, 130

theory, in clinical work 119–21
therapist: aggression towards 27; art 23–5, 45, 47–8, 55–6, 73–4; career of 30–4; good vs. bad 58; locum 12; mistake making by 129–31; as observer 4–5; reflections by 54–6, 64–8, 114–17; role as 'better parent' 9–10, 21, 37–43, 116, 123; as saviour 5; story of Jane's therapy by 3–30; subjectivity of 2; survival of 122–3
therapy: accounts of 21; art 22–6, 36, 45–57, 86; beginning of the ending in 96–9; better mother 37–43, 116, 123; changes reflected in letters 87–90; chronology of 34–6; commitment to 130; conflict in 62–3; contribution of letters to 14–18; crisis precipitation in 26–7; early phase 37–43; end of second year 18; final crisis 104–8; final phase of 35; first crisis in 12; first phase of 35; first year of 4–12; fourth phase of 35, 62; fourth year of 63, 75; initial meeting 3–4; path to change in 77–82; patient's reflections on 112–14; phone calls in 18–19, 87; post-sessional processing of 85–6; reflections on 54–5, 64–8, 112–17; regular weekly 4–12; replacement conceptualisation of 13–14; resolution of 29–30; road to the end 108–12; role of letters in 14–18, 83–102; second break in 19–20; second phase of 35, 58; second year of 13–14; session notes 50–4, 63–5, 75–7, 105; supervision notes 54–6, 80; supervision of 20–2, 27, 36, 66–7, 69–82, 112, 130; taping of 21; theoretical ideas supporting 119–32; therapist's story of 1–3; third phase of 35, 62; third year of 20–2; transformational 114; turning point in 26–30; unanswered question on 131; use of object in 33, 66–7, 97,

101, 116, 121–5, 131; using yourself in 132
trainers 4–5, 32
Transactional Analysis (TA) 8, 32–3, 72, 82, 115; re-parenting in 9, 71; Relational 73
transference 5, 34, 36–7, 43; changing of 57–68, 106–8; instantaneous 115; negative 38, 79, 121, 131; positive 68, 70; re-enactment 97
trust 93

unconscious processes 72–3
unendurable agonies 77–8, 81, 127

van der Hart, Onno 128–9
violence 35, 81; hidden 5–6; images of 60, 76–7; in letters 17, 77; in marriage 110; of patient 28–9, 116

Winnicott, Donald 29, 33, 35, 66–7, 71, 77–8, 81, 87, 98, 101, 117, 121–2, 127–8
work: changing view under supervision 73–5; finishing the 103–17; with 'You and I' 132
workshop 4–5
Wright, Ken 75–6
writing 126–7